WITHDRAWN

Population, Economy, and Society
in Pre-Industrial England

This book is based on the Kent Co-operative
Endowment lectures, second annual series,
delivered in the University of Kent
at Canterbury in May 1967

14 . 10 77

J. D. CHAMBERS

Population, Economy, and Society in Pre-Industrial England

EDITED WITH A PREFACE AND INTRODUCTION BY
W. A. ARMSTRONG

OXFORD UNIVERSITY PRESS
London   Oxford   New York
1972

Oxford University Press

GLASGOW NEW YORK TORONTO MELBOURNE WELLINGTON
CAPE TOWN IBADAN NAIROBI DAR ES SALAAM LUSAKA ADDIS ABABA
DELHI BOMBAY CALCUTTA MADRAS KARACHI LAHORE DACCA
KUALA LUMPUR SINGAPORE HONG KONG TOKYO

PRINTED IN GREAT BRITAIN BY
BUTLER & TANNER LTD
FROME AND LONDON

Preface

JONATHAN DAVID CHAMBERS, Emeritus Professor of Economic and Social History at the University of Nottingham, died in March 1970. Tribute has already been paid to his gifts as an outstanding researcher and teacher in the *festschrift* entitled *Land, labour and population* (eds E. L. Jones and G. E. Mingay, 1967), and more recently, on the sad occasion of his death, by E. A. Wrigley, who writes:

At his death David Chambers' academic reputation stood at a peak. He was one of the most eminent pioneers of methods of attacking historical problems which have spread rapidly during the last fifteen years. . . . Chambers possessed a wide range of talents, at home both in theory and with the tangled intricacies of source materials, able to deal equally felicitously with agriculture and industry, with society as well as economy, with the family as well as the firm, and above all, able to use local materials with brilliant effectiveness. . . . The passing years increased his scope and excellence. He will be missed by a very wide range of historians from the most eminent to the part-time enthusiast, and missed more keenly than in his modesty he would have thought possible. (*Local Population Studies Magazine and Newsletter*, No. 4, Spring 1970, pp. 8–9.)

It is a sign of his remarkable and undiminished intellectual vigour that this book is his third posthumous publication. *Population, Economy, and Society in Pre-Industrial England* is based on a series of lectures delivered at the University of Kent in May 1967. Thereafter, Chambers repeatedly revised and reshaped them for publication with the Oxford University Press, but died before the task was completed, leaving behind various drafts for each chapter, written at different points of time and to some extent overlapping in content. My tasks have included locating what appeared to be the latest versions among his voluminous papers and correspondence, transposing some material between chapters, and re-writing certain sections with a view to clarification. One or two 'inconsistencies', or what might be read as such, inevitably remain: in particular, the latest draft of Chapter 1 takes account of Professor J. F. D. Shrewsbury's *History of the bubonic plague in the British Isles* (1970), while Chapter 4, in dealing with plague, does not. Evidently Chapter 4 was written at an earlier date, but I have not altered it, on the grounds that the essential point which Chambers is making—that variations in the incidence of disease (whether plague or otherwise) constituted an independent factor—is substantially unaffected. Nothing of significance has been added to the content of the draft chapters, and no attempt has been made to modify the arguments therein expressed. Indeed, those who have known the pleasure of his conversation and instruction will at once recognize that the broad architecture of the volume is authentic 'Chambers', reflecting closely the trend of his thinking in recent years.

Referencing has been carried out as fully as an interpretative study of this kind would seem to warrant. All the main citations that the student of population history will require are given, but in the interest of early publication, I have not thought it necessary to go to the trouble of tracing every reference to anecdotal or illustrative material.

A word of explanation respecting the structure of the book may be helpful for those approaching this field of study for the first time. Chapter 1 introduces a number of themes which are subsequently developed in more detail. Chapters 2 and 3 deal with marriage patterns and fertility trends, matters that have been lightly dealt with by historians until comparatively recently. The first of these emphasizes the 'uniqueness of the European marriage pattern', in Professor Hajnal's phrase, a characteristic that impressed Chambers immensely in relation to other factors of economic growth in the West; while the second assesses the significance of recent evidence on short and medium-term oscillations in these variables as they operated within this framework of institutions and conventions. Chapter 4 discusses another issue with which Chambers was highly preoccupied—the idea that fluctuations in mortality did not automatically reflect the immediate availability of resources (especially food, as Malthusians tend to assume), but rather, were caused independently by random (i.e. non-economic) changes in the incidence of epidemic disease. Chambers was perhaps the first modern English historian to espouse this view (in *The Vale of Trent*, 1957), just as the same argument, in its essentials, was being propounded for Scandinavia by Professor Utterström. Historians appear to be increasingly accepting the validity of this view, at least in so far as England and Scandinavia are concerned. As this volume goes to the press, a new article on the causes of fluctuations in nineteenth-century Finnish mortality by E. Jutikkala and M. Kauppinen (*Population Studies*, 25, 1971), appears to give it further confirmation, and no doubt would have afforded the author much satisfaction.

Chapter 5 is more narrowly confined to charting eighteenth-century developments, and may be read as a contribution to the traditional controversy over the immediate demographic causes of the decisive upturn of population at about the mid-century mark. Finally, Chapter 6 returns to the broad issues raised in the first chapter, and reflects on the significance of the connections between population growth and economic development in general terms.

Chambers prepared various rough notes for an introduction to this volume, and I have based the present introduction upon what has survived. Among this material was a passage in which Chambers explained the object of his book:

Since the subject is now studied in university and extra-mural classes and by private individuals in different parts of the country, a general discussion of the historical, as distinct from the technical problems involved, might be expected to be of value. . . . Such an inquiry could rightly be said to be not only premature but impertinent if it laid claim to finality in regard to its findings; but no such claim is made here.

This is perhaps a little too modest in tone. Certainly, any synthesis of existing knowledge in this rapidly developing field must be provisional in character; nevertheless, at the time of writing no other historian has been bold enough to essay a survey of this scope and nature, and few scholars would be as well equipped to do so as Professor Chambers. *Population, Economy, and Society in Pre-Industrial England* will serve as a suitable introduction for students for some years to come, but this is not the full measure of its significance. For in this field the reader is soon carried to the frontiers of knowledge, and this book will be seen to contain a number of fresh hypotheses which should serve to inspire another generation of researchers. Such a claim cannot be made for the generality of student texts, but is by no means extravagant in this case.

W. A. ARMSTRONG

Eliot College,
University of Kent at Canterbury,
September 1971.

Acknowledgements

A GENERAL acknowledgement is due to the following authors and publishers of works containing statistical material presented here in graphical form: W. A. Armstrong (Fig. 3); Edward Arnold Ltd (Tables 4 and 8 and Fig. 3); The Athlone Press (Table 9 and Fig. 5b); Basic Books Inc. (Table 1); Cambridge University Press (Tables 3, 9, 10, 13, 14 and Fig. 5a); Frank Cass & Co. Ltd (Tables 6 11 and 12); the Editor of the *Economic History Review* and Professor G. S. L. Tucker (Fig. 4); Methuen & Co. Ltd (Table 7); Mr N. Tranter (Table 5) and Weidenfeld & Nicolson Ltd (Table 1). I have indicated the sources of information in each case. Dr F. West has kindly permitted citation of unpublished results from his study of Wrangle (pp. 46, 97–8). There are a few references to the results of unpublished aggregative work on Bedfordshire and Lancashire parish registers (pp. 135, 148), where the author enjoyed the co-operation of Mr F. G. Emmison of the Essex County Record Office, and the Cambridge Group for the History of Population and Social Structure respectively. Mrs A. Widdowson of the University of Nottingham calculated the correlation coefficients referred to on p. 96, and Professor C. W. J. Granger freely gave advice on statistical matters whenever necessary.

There will be many others whose assistance Professor Chambers, indefatigable and enthusiastic correspondent as he was, would have liked to have acknowledged by name, but their specific contributions to his thinking are less easy to trace. For my own part I should like to thank Dr W. H. Chaloner, Mr V. H. T. Skipp, Dr R. S. Smith, Dr N. L. Tranter, and Dr J. Z. Titow for answering postal queries relating to sources, as well as the secretaries of my college for cheerful and excellent service, and the staff of the Clarendon Press, especially for re-drawing the diagrams.

W. A. A.

Contents

List of Figures

List of Tables

Introduction

T HE modern study of population history in England can be traced to two sources. On the empirical side, it begins with the work of John Rickman, the originator and architect of five successive censuses between 1801 and 1841. He had written a paper in 1796 entitled 'Thoughts on the Utility and Facility of a General Enumeration of the People of the British Empire', setting out the economic advantages of 'ascertaining the number of the population . . . and the facility of arithmetically deducing it from the parish registers' (Williams, p. 40). This paper was communicated by Mr George Rose, M.P. for Christchurch, to Charles Abbot, the future Speaker of the House of Commons, who, as a result, introduced the Population Bill in 1800. Once it was passed, Abbot offered the supervision of the returns to Rickman. 'It is a task of national benefit', the latter wrote, 'and I should be fanciful to reject it, because offered by rogues.' His suspicion that the office was a bribe was probably unfounded, since Abbott shortly afterwards offered him the post of Secretary, which, with other offices, he occupied for the next forty years. At all events, Rickman, a fanatically honest man, determined to avoid the suspicion of robbery and corruption by 'doing the business well, and taking no more remuncration than I judge exactly adequate to the trouble' (Williams, pp. 38, 40). His remuneration was, in fact, 500 guineas, out of which he had to pay his clerks and meet various expenses; not surprisingly, he found himself out of pocket when 'the business' was over.

Rickman was given an office in the Cockpit, off Birdcage Walk, where he was occupied more or less continuously for many years. Here, in 1801, with the slenderest resources, he embarked upon the compilation of the census returns which remain the essential starting-point of population inquiries for the period 1801–41. The returns included information as to the number of inhabited and uninhabited houses in each of the 11,000 parishes of the country; the number of families inhabiting each house; the number of persons in each parish on the day of the inquiry, as well as the number of persons engaged in trade and manufacture, and in agriculture. In addition, each census down to 1841 was accompanied by a *Parish Register Abstract*. That of 1801 summarized the number of baptisms and burials in every tenth year from 1700 to 1780, and each year between 1780 and 1800; together with annual totals for marriages between 1754 and 1800. This information was elicited from the clergy, the censal data being the work of overseers of the poor at the local level. From these sources Rickman himself made two sets of estimates of the total population at ten-yearly intervals from 1700 to 1780 and at five-yearly intervals. thereafter, whilst John Finlaison, an actuary in the National Debt Office of the Treasury made another, which accompanied the 1831 census. In 1841 Rickman accomplished the biggest inquiry so far attempted in the field of historical demography by asking the clergy for details of baptisms and burials for the years 1570, 1600, 1630, 1700, and 1750, where the necessary registers existed; on this basis he calculated the population of England as a whole in these years. Rickman died in 1841 and, after the usual obituary salutations, was virtually forgotten. Although the decadal censuses continued and expanded into a great national service, his pioneering work on historical demography was not followed up, apart from two exercises in this field by William Farr, a senior official in the Registrar-General's Office, in the censuses of 1861 and 1871. It would not be too strong to say that on the empirical side, the study of historical population trends remained in a state of suspended animation for nearly a hundred years.

Modern developments on the theoretical side were initiated by T. R. Malthus in his *Essay on the Principle of Population as it affects the future improvement of society*, first published in 1798, which took possession of the imagination of his contemporaries and has continued to reverberate around the world to the present time. Thomas Malthus was born in 1766, and educated in the first instance by his father Daniel. The parent was a retiring, scholarly man, yet noted for the liberality of his views and wide circle of enlightened acquaintances, which included Rousseau, for whom Daniel Malthus acted as an executor. Philosophical questions were constantly under discussion in such a household, and it was in response to his father's championship of the optimistic views of human nature and progress set forth by Godwin, Condorcet, and other utopians, that young Thomas was moved to set down his ideas on paper. Professing to have read some of the various speculations on the future improvement of society, 'in a temper very different from a wish to find them visionary', he asserted that population dynamics were the strongest obstacle impeding the future perfectibility of society. Briefly stated, the Malthusian principle of population may be reduced to the following propositions:

1. The passion between the sexes is innate and unchanging, and tends to produce population growth at a geometrical rate (1, 2, 4, 8, etc.)

2. The resources to support population can only be added to at a slower rate. (Malthus stressed subsistence in the form of food, and argued that an arithmetical growth rate, 1, 2, 3, 4, etc., would be the best that could ordinarily be anticipated.)

3. Population has, therefore, an inherent *tendency* to outrun resources; an equilibrium is secured by the operation of the following 'checks', which to a certain extent are alternatives:

(a) positive checks: summarized as famine, misery, wars, and 'vice', operating on the death-rate directly and through attendant disease.

(b) preventive or prudential checks: that is, *not* birth control (which Malthus did not anticipate, and which he would have classed as a form of 'vice'), but delayed, or prudential marriage.

The preventive check was given heavier emphasis in the second edition of the essay (1803), without any major concessions at other points in the structure of the argument; in addition Malthus provided a great deal more supporting 'evidence' from a variety of sources, although it was often distorted in order to support the argument (Smith, pp. 220, 256–71).

Although these views were rejected by some of the leading thinkers of the day, for example, Nassau Senior and Edwin

Chadwick, both of whom rebutted the charge of being Malthusians (Glass, 1953, p. 6), they were incorporated into the structure of classical economics and invested with the authority of a social 'law' before which every proposal of social policy or item of public expenditure had to prove its case. In alliance with the principle of diminishing returns to investment in agriculture and the wage-fund theory, the Malthusian argument appeared for many years impregnable, and retained its hold over most economists until the time of Alfred Marshall.

Although the two were contemporaries, Malthus and Rickman ran parallel but separate courses which never met; Malthus largely ignored the empirical work of Rickman and, in turn, Rickman deplored the social implications of the Malthusian population theory as they threatened to work themselves out in the context of the reform of the English Poor Law (Williams, p. 167). Even so, for a century these men stamped the subject with their characteristic methods and attitudes with such strength that to attempt to challenge their findings appeared to historians, if not impious, at least impracticable. This was partly due to the inherent difficulties of the material and relative inaccessibility of the evidence, scattered as it is in the strong-boxes of 11,000 parishes and other repositories, and replete with the statistical problems inseparable from material so haphazardly collected and preserved. Subsequent historians such as Gonner (1913), Buer (1926), and Griffith (1926: second edn 1967), simply based themselves on Rickman's *Parish Register Abstracts*, unsatisfactory though these were. Yet historians are not lacking in skill and pertinacity, and we can only conclude that their failure to make more of the parish registers owed much to the theoretical context within which population study was generally undertaken. From the time of Malthus onwards the study of population was regarded as a branch of economics, and its 'laws' were laid down with such logical force and apparent precision, that empirical inquiry at the grass-roots level seemed unnecessary. The Malthusian formula appeared to fit all the facts everywhere, at least for pre-industrial times, and it was unthinkable that the rude entries made by generations of parish clerks and incumbents had any contribution to make to this august structure of thought. Even today historians are apt to give the theory a sympathetic hearing as a reasonable approximation to the facts of life in pre-industrial times. Thus Professor Cipolla has observed:

If one looked at the population before the Industrial Revolution one got the impression that it was held in the 'Malthusian trap'. Whatever the country, one found that the gross birth rate was usually about 30–55 per thousand. With death rates at around 25–35 per thousand, this gave one a population growth rate of 0·5–1·5 per cent per annum. But this growth soon ran into difficulties and a peak in the death rate eliminated a high percentage of the population' . . . One could argue that Malthus was basically right . . . Thanks to the Industrial Revolution, the European population was able to escape the Malthusian trap (Rostow, p. 401).

Whether or not the Malthusian framework of analysis is thought adequate as an explanation of population trends in pre-industrial society (and this book will assail that view), it has seemed to many to be very apposite to the situation in which present-day under-developed countries find themselves—that is, a vicious circle of self-perpetuating poverty as a result of the pressure of population against resources. The questions that occur to historians in any age are apt to be influenced by the pressing issues of their own times, and much of the renewed interest in the historical population trends of the West is derived from the post-war preoccupation with developmental studies. How did Western Europe embark upon the path of self-sustained economic growth? What was the nature of the old regime from which it escaped? What parallels exist with the modern underdeveloped world, and can the historian isolate the key changes in such a way as to enable practical lessons to be drawn?

Such questions have tended to be very much at the forefront of the minds of the post-war generation of economic and social historians; that is to say, of the kind of historian who is in any case predisposed to study the everyday patterns of life of ordinary people, as against the political and diplomatic affairs of the great.

In the field of English population history, further work has been carried out on the Rickman *Parish Register Abstracts* (see Deane and Cole, 1962), and a number of notable regional studies based on aggregative methods (i.e. the simple counting of entries of baptisms, burials, and marriages) have appeared (see especially Chambers, 1957 and 1960, Eversley, 1965, Drake, 1962, Pentland, 1965, and for a valuable inventory, Hollingsworth, 1969). Many interpretative essays have appeared and, to a limited extent, well-known sources have been re-examined with population questions in mind.

However, the latest techniques, those of family reconstitution, differ only in scope and purpose from the methods long employed by genealogists and antiquarians. The essence of the technique is to evaluate the demographic experience of successive generations in traceable families, by relating entries of births, deaths, and marriages in a parish register, so circumventing the difficulty that the *total* population of the community in question is not generally known before 1801 (in effect, the researcher builds up his own 'population' for study), and permitting the calculation of more refined demographic indices, such as age-specific fertility and mortality rates. In a word, the method allows for greater precision and detail (depth as against breadth) than is possible through earlier approaches. The family reconstitution method was pioneered by M. Henry and his colleagues in France, where the state of the registers is generally superior and where there has been an especially long-standing concern with historical population questions, arising out of the extraordinarily early and protracted fall in French fertility (see below, p. 71). Latterly the technique has been applied to a number of English parishes (see especially Wrigley, 1966, and Tranter, 1966); and to special social groups where the necessary data exist (Hollingsworth, 1964). Indeed, further researches of this nature are high on the list of priorities of the Cambridge Group for the History of Population and Social Structure, formed by Dr Wrigley and Mr Laslett in 1964.

Many interesting findings have come to light as a result of recent researches, and will be surveyed in this book. Amongst the most interesting are the apparently comparatively late age at marriage which has always characterized Western Europe, a sharp contrast with the situation elsewhere; that pre-industrial populations did not, apparently, breed to anything like the biological maximum and exercised a degree of control or choice in the matter of fertility; and that mortality statistics did not, as the Malthusian theory implies, bear a close and direct relationship with the availability of resources, as measured by food prices.

Enough is already known to show that the study of population change cannot be circumscribed within conventional economic categories, and that religious, biological, and perhaps psychological factors will need to be taken into account. In so far as the economic interpretation of population growth is weakened by consideration of such factors, we are driven to conceding an independent role to population change as an autonomous variable, a cause rather than an effect, exercising an important influence on the economy during periods of advance as well as stagnation. That is the point of view expressed in this book.

W. A. A.

1

The General Course of Population Change, 1086 - 1801

(A) FACTORS IN POPULATION CHANGE

One result of the revived interest in the study of economic growth is the deference that historians are willing to pay to population as a factor in the course of economic change. No general economic history is likely to be attempted today without reference to the demographic background within which economic change took place, and it is a striking tribute to the pervasive influence of the Malthusian view that the context within which the discussion is usually presented remains fundamentally unaltered. The latest example is Dr Brenner's *Short History of Economic Progress* in which the author opens with a citation from the master himself in his most uncompromising vein. 'For centuries', says Brenner, 'mankind has been living on the borderline of starvation. Malthus lays this on "the constant tendency of all animated life to increase beyond the nourishment prepared for it" ' (p. 1). There was a moving equilibrium, he writes, between the rate of population growth and its means of subsistence.

Whenever, in relation to population, land was abundant, birthrates rose in excess of deathrates and people became more numerous. But when the accretion of people reached the limit of 'the nourishment prepared for it' (at the prevailing level of technology) and poorer land was put to use diminishing returns from land set in. Sooner or later the population growth abated and the trend reversed (p. 5).

A second example which might be cited is the more subtle reference by Professor Landes in his rightly acclaimed chapter on the Industrial Revolution in the *Cambridge Economic History* (1965). He writes (p. 274): 'An amelioration of the conditions of existence, hence of survival, and an increase in economic opportunity had *always* [my italics] been followed by a rise in population that eventually consumed the gains achieved.'

It would seem to follow from these expositions of the general theory of population growth that England should have been the land where growth was most rapid. Equipped as it was with an agriculture that, from the late seventeenth century, regularly produced a surplus over the needs of the country, an expanding industry, and a flourishing trade, a stable government, and an unprecedented freedom of person and exchange, what more was needed to provide 'an amelioration of the condition of existence'? Yet it does not seem to have been followed by a corresponding increase of population. In his recent *Population and History* (p. 153) Dr Wrigley provides the following figures (Table 1):

TABLE 1

Eighteenth-century Population Growth Rates

(percentage per annum)

England and Wales	1701–1801	0·45	East Prussia	1700–1800	0·84
Italy	1700–1800	0·45	Pomerania	1740–1800	0·80
Sweden	1749–1800	0·59	Silesia	1740–1804	0·94
Württemburg	1740–1800	0·56	Austria	1754–89	0·94
France	1700–89	0·31	Bohemia	1754–89	1·18
France	1740–89	0·45	Hungary	1754–89	3·01

He goes on to say:

In a number of European countries population growth in the eighteenth century was very swift by the general standards of pre-industrial societies, and was often at its swiftest in areas most remote from rapid economic change. Rates of growth as high as those in England occurred in many parts of Europe, and in many countries there was an acceleration . . . about the middle of the century (p. 152).

The factor sometimes held responsible for this has been the intro-duction of the potato into the diet of the poor, but this supposition has some difficulties to overcome. A useful summary of the litera-ture on it has been given by Van Bath who writes (p. 268):

In France the Royal Family and ministers went to great trouble to encourage the eating of potatoes. They were served at the royal table and Queen Marie Antoinette wore the flowers as a corsage; but all this effort bore little fruit. The French shunned the strange new vegetable. In Germany, too, it was not until the second half of the eighteenth century that potato growing spread from market garden to farm. By 1719 potatoes were already of some importance and during the famine years 1770–2 they came into general use.

It would seem from this that the initiation of the European rise of population was anterior to the general rise of the potato in the popular dietary, and that we are tempted to fall back on another factor which was common to the area: the cessation of plague in epidemic form from about 1720. Professor Helleiner has succinctly summarized the factors at work in his essay 'The Vital Revolution Reconsidered':

Though the rates of growth varied widely from country to country, the population was on the increase everywhere from 1720 onwards . . . most students of the history of population seem to agree that a significant reduction in mortality was the primary cause of the demographic upswings; . . . we should argue however that it was the peaks rather than the plateau of mortality that were lowered. In other words, it was not so much a reduction in mortality in 'normal' years that produced the secular downward trend of the death rate, but an unmistakeable abatement of the 'great crises'. The disappearance of plague, above all, but also a very sensible mitigation of subsistence crises seem to have been chiefly responsible for the increase in life expectancy (Glass and Eversley, p. 85).

To which Helleiner adds a rider, 'that subsistence crises, unlike those of previous centuries, could no longer raise the spectre of plague had, of course, a great deal to do with this attenuation'.

The only point at which I would wish to diverge from this admirable statement is when he goes on to account for this fundamental shift in the balance of forces making for high mortality. 'However,' he says (p. 86), 'when all is said an obscure ecological revolution among rodents—the disappearance of the black rat— which we believe to have been responsible for the cessation of plague in Europe must be given its due.' It should be noted, however, that L. F. Hirst, whom he cites in support of this view, also introduces another factor which Helleiner seems to have overlooked. In his *Conquest of Plague*, after discussing the ecological question of the replacement of the black rat by the brown rat, he goes on to present a learned disquisition on the neglected subject of mutation as a factor in the decline of plague; and concludes (p. 338):

The change of rodent species, by itself [i.e. from black rat to brown rat], therefore, cannot account for the failure of the disease to spread actively among rural and urban European rats. When, however, the change of rat species is associated with a change in flea species, we have an adequate explanation of the relative immunity of Western Europe from plague in modern times.

The vital revolution was thus, on the continent of Europe, at least as much a response to biological as to economic factors; but what of England? Here the plague disappeared in 1666, half a century before its disappearance from continental Europe, yet the demographic response was strangely muted. Professor Shrewsbury has recently insisted that the plague should not be saddled with more than its fair share of responsibility for mortality (pp. 36, 104, 478), and its demise was in any case followed by a variety of afflictions which were scarcely less destructive of life, as Creighton's *History of Epidemics* so amply shows. While the plague had been 'peculiarly fatal to adult lives', the tendency was, if anything, for the mortality from infectious diseases to fall 'in much the larger ratio upon infants and children' (ii. 18). At all events, there can be no doubt, in view of the gathering strength of the economy, especially on the agricultural side, that the biological factor—even in the absence of plague—was the most important single influence in holding back the rate of population growth at the time when all the economic signals were set fair for speedy advance. The vital revolution in England came no sooner—if as soon—as on the continent: but when it came, it advanced with an *élan* which carried it, by the end of the eighteenth century, to the head of the pack.

Seen in this context of the comparative growth of European population, the long-term pattern of English demographic change assumes a new significance. Instead of being a slow, almost stagnant, upward movement in obedience to the gathering strength of the economy, as it is often assumed to have been, it is seen as a fluctuating curve alternating between periods of growth and stagnation (indeed decline and recovery), owing strangely little allegiance to contemporary secular economic change; and the net change between the high-water mark of the Middle Ages and the mid-eighteenth century was surprisingly small in view of the varied and substantial progress of the economy (see Figure 1).

It should of course be remembered that the long-term movement of population which we are discussing here was a general trend around which short-term movements oscillated with different and sometimes contradictory local and even national effects. The two main causes of these were localized harvest failures, usually but not always associated with epidemic outbreaks. A bad harvest which was not mitigated by stored-up or alternative supplies of food would have immediate effects on the mortality rates of what has been termed the 'harvest sensitive' group of the population, and endemic health hazards would be aggravated especially among children, perhaps to epidemic proportions. A succession of two or three bad harvests might have devastating effects over a wide area especially if they were accompanied by a crisis of public health. Even a single harvest failure would immediately tend to shift the schedule of demand of the poor from industrial products to food products, and this effect would be felt in ever-widening circles as the shortage continued, especially if the victims had to resort to the consumption of their seed corn. How far these effects would follow from the direct impact of food shortage acting alone cannot be measured, but it is important to emphasize that the presence or absence of the agent of disease might be a deciding factor. As Major Greenwood has observed in regard to the spread of typhus in Ireland in the nineteenth century, 'even in a starving and over-crowded population, if the *materies morbi* is not widely dissemin-ated an epidemic may not be generated' (p. 178). On the other hand, the biological factor could bring utter disaster with or without the accompanying factor of acute food shortage. The circumstances immediately preceding the Black Death provide a striking example. It came at the end of a series of relatively good harvests and moderate prices and must be regarded as the classic case of the action of the autonomous death-rate. For, to quote the most recent study:

These [1325–45] were fortunate years of favourable weather and good harvests. The population was recovering from a temporary check in the Great Famine [of 1315–17] and the peasants were actively exploiting their opportunities. More land was under cultivation, and even marginal land was productive in good seasons; . . . a run of bad weather and poor harvests would have brought another period of dearth and perhaps a Malthusian situation; but it does not seem to me that a Malthusian situation already existed in 1340. The prospective ghost of Malthus stalked only in 1348–9 (Watts, p. 547).

It was anticipated by the Black Death that fell like a thunderbolt from a relatively clear sky: a striking example of the quite disproportionate effect of the factor of epidemic disease in a situation that is only 'prospectively' Malthusian.

The Great Plague inaugurated a century of stagnating rates of growth, although no doubt many examples of short-term recovery which temporarily reversed the trend might be cited, if the necessary local data were available. But there seems to be no doubt that a new departure in the national trend did not appear for over a hundred years, at some point between 1450 and 1470, from which period a phase of rising population is distinguishable until about 1620–40. This similarly was liable to sudden interruptions by short-term crises which could temporarily reverse the trend. One such was the pandemic of influenza preceded by famine that swept over Europe in 1557–8 with important effects on both population and prices. Professor Fisher has recently suggested (1965, p. 127), that it may have reduced the population by almost 20 per cent and 'the wage-earning population by an even greater proportion since the ranks of the wage-earners would be thinned not only by death but also by movement to replenish the diminished number of husbandmen and employers'. Even if the reduction was much smaller than this, it would have been sufficient, he thinks, to effect an upward turn in wage rates, and by the 1560s in some parts of the country they were double what they had been at the end of the fifteenth century. At the same time, the upswing of prices had faltered and 'was not renewed until the 1570s, long before there was any concrete evidence of renewed monetary inflation'; a response, he suggests, to the recovery of population growth, which appears to have been renewed in the 1570s (p. 124). By the 1590s it could be taken as a matter of common knowledge. Population change, instead of behaving as a passive variable reflecting food and/or employment opportunities is here seen as an independent factor acting on the market through the force of demand for the products of agriculture.

Many examples of short-term crises arising mainly from harvest failures could of course be cited; but, except for the terrible famine of 1315–17 they appear to have been localized in their effects.

Professor Drake has called attention to the widening radius of disaster originating in food crises in 1622–3 among the weavers of the West Riding who would have additional burdens of unemployment as a result of the shifting schedule of demand from goods for food, and he points out that if, as he assumed was the case, disease was also present, vagrants would act as carriers of infection when they wandered into neighbouring areas in search of food (p. 436). No doubt such local crises were common in pre-industrial times, and where there was a thickening of population density to the point at which urban conditions could be said to obtain, the upward movement of the burial rate would be further enhanced as a result of closer contact and the congestion which facilitated infection.

In such circumstances, the conditions described by M. Goubert for the Beauvaisis might be expected to have obtained in England. Wheat prices, he says, could be taken in that area as 'a veritable demographic barometer' through their effects upon mortality and hence on marriages and births (1952, p. 468). But how far the same can be said of England as a whole is difficult to establish. Probably Professor Drake's example of the West Riding could be paralleled in many parts of northern England in the seventeenth century, and unpublished evidence suggests that these conditions may have sometimes prevailed in the large straggling parishes of Lancashire and the Border country up to the end of that century; but there has been singularly little confirmation of this supposition in the country as a whole or in the large urban centres, especially London. M. Goubert's grim picture of direct Malthusian response of demographic variables to harvest conditions no doubt had its localized exemplars but it is not obviously reflected in the long-term national pattern.

The situation in England seems to have been more complicated than this: high prices encouraged high mortality but did not usually induce mortality crises. To do this they had to be allied to epidemic outbreaks. Fertility, too, might be checked, but not, if the example of Colyton is typical, in response to rising prices; 'homeostatic techniques of adjustment', to use Dr Wrigley's term, were certainly applied 'so that the worst seldom if ever happened'. But in the example he cites it seems to have been used *after* the crisis was over, not to stave it off (see Chapter 3).

The outstanding factor that emerges from this inquiry is the biological one, the utter dependence of the pre-industrial population, even in the absence of Malthusian pressures, on the fortuitous movement of natural forces which could wipe out not merely local but national surpluses in a few disastrous months; or by a similarly fortuitous combination of circumstances lift the burden of disease and permit growth to the point at which the ameliorative conditions were in danger of being wiped out by over-rapid advance.

That this actually happened on a national scale in England is a supposition that has not been fully established by empirical research though it is generally implied. The social crisis in the closing years of the Tudor period is usually cited as one such example. In terms of real wages ameliorative conditions for the mass of consumers would certainly appear to have been wiped out; but, in order to identify a meaningful demographic crisis, we would expect to encounter fewer and later marriages, lower birthrates, and higher death-rates. In the Devonshire village of Colyton, the only example for which we have the necessary data, none of these conditions obtained. Between 1590 and 1600, marriages were climbing to a peak; a fall followed to 1620, and then there occurred a further rapid rise. Births followed an even more consistent upward course in 1630 and burials actually fell between 1590 and 1600 and remained at a low level for twenty years (Wrigley, 1969, p. 82). Dr Wrigley himself expressly notes the absence of Malthusian demographic characteristics for this period, and charges it to the insensitivity of the people's reaction to changes in their economic condition. He writes:

If marriage decisions in Colyton had reflected sensitively the changes in real income average age at first marriage of women should have tended to rise during the sixteenth century as population pressure grew. After the middle of the seventeenth century the average age should have tended to fall again. In fact, matters turned out quite differently (1969, pp. 141–2).

Wrigley explains this on the ground that this is an example of a 'lurch', i.e. a postponement of the Malthusian response to a subsequent period when the Malthusian cause no longer applied. Whether this speculation is valid, further research will no doubt show; but it would not be difficult to argue that the flattening out of the population curve in the second half of the seventeenth century could have been more convincingly explained by the ravages of plague, smallpox, and other diseases than to the pressure of population which in fact was actually falling.

If there is no clear evidence of a Malthusian crisis on the demographic side in the height of the Elizabethan food crisis, was there one on the economic side in the form of a cut-back of production owing to the failure of demand as a result of mass poverty? In view of the claims that have been made for agriculture, industry, and trade in this period it is difficult to believe there was a global fall in output even though there seems to have been a drastic fall in real income *per capita*.

On this aspect of Malthusian crisis, Professor Habbakuk sheds a clarifying gleam of light (1958, pp. 30–1). The positive effects of population growth could outweigh the negative only in an economy having access to a high rate of savings, an abundant supply of productive land either at home or overseas, and a class of experienced entrepreneurs. These conditions were obviously lacking in the great upward surge of the thirteenth century, when land resources in the context of the techniques of the time were patently overstretched, yields showed signs of decline, and the 'harvest sensitive' group closely reflected the changes in the price of grain in their rising death-rates; while the rise of population seems to have been definitely checked. But conditions in Tudor England were very different; and it is difficult to see where they fell short of Professor Habbakuk's conditions under which the positive effects of population growth could outweigh the negative.

It is true, Professor Fisher has spoken of 'an economy in which agriculture was not expanding sufficiently to provide men with all the food, the farms and the employment they needed and in which industrial development was too slow to make up for the deficiencies of agriculture' (1957, p. 16). The demographic explosion may have been such as to justify this gloomy and essentially Malthusian picture, yet it is difficult to reconcile it with the ecstatic account of the progress of agriculture described by Dr Kerridge, and if there was a Malthusian crisis it was evidently of short duration. Kerridge writes (p. 344):

Rents and prices rose to a peak in the 1610s, but the nation then had its first glimpse of the horrors of plenty, *of that avalanche of goods that follows great innovations* [my italics] and crashes through the old price structure. Rents which had risen threefold, suddenly broke. By 1620, corn prices were less than two thirds the 31 year mean . . . No very dear year had occurred since 1613, and the consequence was, in 1621 some capital farmers had as much as five years' corn in store.

Perhaps a factor contributing to this startling change was the return of the epidemic cycle, especially of the plague which raised mortality and cut back consumption. As in the 1340s, the ghost of Malthus may have stalked prospectively; but it was once again anticipated by the demographic factor which continued to exercise a depressing effect until about the end of the seventeenth century.

If, as I am suggesting, the assumption of a Malthusian check in the late sixteenth and early seventeenth centuries remains unproven it would seem possible to argue that except for the demographic crisis of the late thirteenth century, the changing balance between population and resources in England did not induce economic retreat, either on the upswing or the downswing, so that continuous growth in each demographic phase was possible: the upswings yielded a stimulation of aggregate production, a form of profit inflation at the cost of *per capita* income but not such as to produce a cutback either of national population or total production; and on the downswings, *per capita* income accumulated, making funds available for saving and spending when the next phase of demographic advance gave the initial stimulus of cheap labour to sustain it. Thus, population change instead of producing periodic retardation, as it is assumed to have done through Malthusian crises, may itself have been a factor behind continuous growth in England at least from the Middle Ages. But it should be remembered that it performed this role in the especially favourable conditions that obtained there: an island economy, free from destructive wars, with a relatively equitable tax structure which

---

FIG. 1: Population and Wheat Prices, 1100–1800

Figure 1 was drawn up by Professor Chambers, on the basis of the following data:

Prices: Postan and Titow (1961) and Hoskins (1968), with interpolation using W. G. Hoskins, 'Harvest fluctuations and English economic history, 1480–1619', *Agricultural History Review*, 12, 1964; W. H. Beveridge, 'A statistical crime of the seventeenth century', *Journal of Economic and Business History*, 1 (1929); and ibid., *Prices and wages in England from the twelfth to the nineteenth century* (Longmans, London, 1939).

Population: various scattered estimates. The calamitous fall indicated for the second half of the fourteenth century is based on Russell (1948), referred to on p. 84.

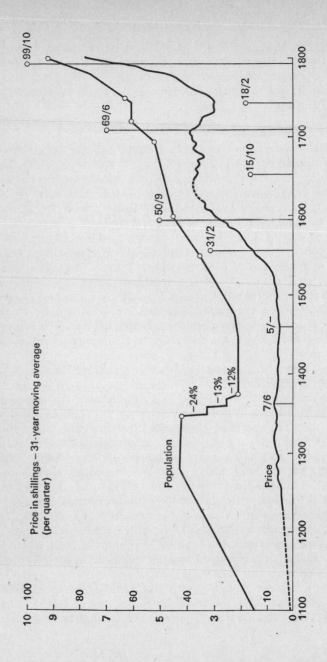

Price in shillings – 31-year moving average (per quarter)

B

placed the burden where it could best be borne, an innovating class that was prepared to make use of these advantages; and perhaps especially an agriculture with an inbuilt propensity for making the best use of the soil through the landlord–tenant system of cultivation.

(b) THE COURSE OF POPULATION CHANGE

I shall now attempt to give a summary of the general pattern of population change in England from Domesday Book to the first census in 1801. This is indeed a difficult and dangerous enterprise. In view of the nature of the evidence—Domesday Book itself, old Tax Returns, Hearth Tax, Subsidy Rolls, Parish Registers, and the like—and the difficulty of interpreting it, there is risk not only of error, but of doing less than justice to the work of those who have contributed so much to this highly specialized and complex field of study; but I think enough is known to make it possible to present, if not a series of agreed global figures, at least an outline of the direction that was probably taken by the course of population change over the period. I propose to set alongside it a thirty-one-year moving average of wheat prices to provide a framework for the general discussion to which the demographic data give rise in section (c).

We begin with the very remarkable rise from Domesday to the end of the thirteenth century, a rise of 300 per cent or more. The causes are generally attributed to the fact that in the late eleventh and early twelfth centuries (and more particularly after 1250) there were few recorded epidemics, thus life expectancy and fertility were probably high. In addition new lands were available and there are some reports of labour shortage, both probably making for earlier marriage. Dr Hollingsworth would put the period of most rapid advance between 1143 and 1173 rather than in the thirteenth century from the evidence of medieval epidemics (1969, p. 387). But whatever the precise dates of the peaks of growth were, the medieval demographic boom seems to have come to an end in southern England by, perhaps, the 1280s when death-rates reached as high as 70 to 75 per thousand in some Winchester estates (Postan and Titow, p. 400).

It will be seen that this period of rapid advance was followed by a catastrophic fall: no less than 50 per cent in fact between the onset of the Black Death in 1348 and the last quarter of the century.

At this point, a warning recently sounded by Professor Shrewsbury should be carefully noted. He points out that the bubonic plague, being carried by the black rat, was preeminently a dwelling-house disease; and very many villages must have escaped because there was no link between the houses; in fact it was 'a biological impossibility for the whole or even a major part of England to have been ravaged by the "Great Pestilence of 1348–50" '. He argues that since three-quarters of the population were living south and east of the York–Exeter axis, a similar proportion of the rat population would be located in that area since it was entirely dependent for accommodation in the British Isles on human habitation. The conclusion is that the plague may have destroyed perhaps one-third of the population in East Anglia and one-twentieth in the rest of England (pp. 24–6, 34–6); although smallpox and typhus could also have been present. Indeed, the rat could transmit typhus to men and the two forms of disease tended to alternate; and when they were joined by dysentery and relapsing fever they were together responsible for the 'famine fevers' which figure so often in pre-industrial demographic crises (pp. 124–5). It would seem therefore that the bubonic plague should not be charged with entire responsibility for the demographic crisis. Going further, Shrewsbury absolves the bubonic plague from the main responsibility for the succession of epidemic outbreaks in the second half of the fourteenth century and also for the persistent outbreaks of the fifteenth. He asks whether the normal outbreaks from 1405 to 1407, for instance, could have been waterborne attacks of cholera or typhus or malignant dysentery or even smallpox? The 1433–4 outbreak, he believes, might well be associated with the disease-carrying proclivities of the house-fly, which swarmed in warm weather, and carried all the infections mentioned; with the addition of bacterial food poisoning, infantile summer diarrhoea, and 'bloody flux', i.e. dysentery. And those of 1444, 1446, 1447–54, 1465, 1471, 1476, and 1478 may perhaps be similarly explained (pp. 144–9).

The reasons for this partial absolution of the bubonic plague for the mortality crises of the fifteenth century are essentially biological. 'The governing factor in the persistence of this disease in England', he says,

was the length of time that an imported strain of *Pasteurella pestis* retained its virulence among the house rats . . . Sooner or later, however, each strain died out spontaneously and the bubonic plague disappeared from the country until a fresh, virulent strain was imported. In the intervals between successive importations, local epidemics affecting individual towns and villages occurred; but the introduction of a fresh strain was required for the production of a major, *national* outburst of bubonic plague, and after 1350 the next outbreak of this magnitude was in my judgement that of 1563 (p. 139).

In some respects, the problem becomes more, not less, baffling as a result of this relative absolution of plague from the main responsibility. Yet we are still faced with the factor of epidemic disease as the main demographic agency, effecting a long-term check to population growth when purely physical conditions would have pointed to the opposite. As Professor Thrupp has observed, 'the period from 1349 to the 1470s, if it was a golden age, was the golden age of bacteria' (p. 118).

That such an era should have come to an end must remain a biological problem; but in so far as population growth is a reflection of bacterial virulence, there must have been some powerful biological influence at work, since there is general agreement that an upward movement can be detected from the later fourteenth century, mounting to another demographic boom in the Tudor period, continuing even through the crisis of subsistence at the end of the century. Perhaps there was a growing immunity among the surviving population; or perhaps a weakening of the strains of the various forms of killing diseases, but there was nothing in the physical environment known to historians that could be held responsible for the change in the directions of the demographic curve.

The long-term upward movement of population, broken from time to time by fierce epidemic attacks—1558, 1563, 1593, 1625— came to an end by the middle of the century. That bubonic plague had returned in strength is accepted on all sides, and the actual enumeration of plague deaths in London and in other towns in the form of Bills of Mortality or similar specific records leave us in no doubt that it was the chief agent of destruction. But the galaxy of diseases mentioned by Shrewsbury was at work with almost equal strength; and when the plague died out in 1666 the ravages of its deadly allies—typhus, smallpox, influenza, malarial ague—reached unprecedented heights and stamped the post-plague period as one of the most destructive of the century.

The next stage, however, is more difficult to establish. I have indicated a sharp rise from the decade 1680 to 1690, slowing down to stagnation pace about 1720 (Figure 1). Whether this would be generally acceptable for the country as a whole is not entirely certain, but for the Midlands and the Home Counties, for Manchester, Liverpool, and Birmingham, and above all London I think there can be no doubt about it, as I shall endeavour to show subsequently. Again, for the sharp check that followed (*circa* 1718–41), epidemic attacks are generally held responsible; not the plague but smallpox, typhus, enteric fevers, and a variety of deadly afflictions as a result of which, in the words of a medical man at Ripon, 'villages were almost stripped of their poor people' (Chambers, 1957, p. 29), and doctors could do nothing to help them. And finally, about 1745 we see the beginning of a renewed upward surge which was the prelude not, as in earlier times, to a return of high death-rates and population stagnation, but a still more pronounced upward movement that marked a breakthrough to a new demographic age.

(c) THE ECONOMIC IMPLICATIONS

In regard to the line in Figure 1 representing the prices of wheat per quarter, I think one very important inference can be drawn, namely that the increases in population tended on the whole to accompany, if not indeed to precede, rises in prices; if this is accepted we must conclude that the long-term growth of population was operating on the economy through the price mechanism as an extraneous factor independent of the economy itself. Of course there were other factors at work such as inflation, bad harvests, and war: but the behaviour of the long-term trend is consistent with the view that the demographic movement may be an independent factor on the price trend at least in the case of three out of four periods of price rise.

We must notice, however, that in one period the relationship between the demographic and the price series calls for a different hypothesis. The period in question is roughly 1650 to 1750, during which it will be seen that while the population series followed a fluctuating but upward trend, the price series took a decided downward plunge until the third quarter of the eighteenth century when once again the earlier association reasserted itself and the steep rise of population was followed by a still steeper rise of prices. If this interpretation of the price-population trend is correct, we may go on to say that in the thirteenth-century boom and in that of the Elizabethan period, and again in the last quarter of the eighteenth century, the movement of population exercised a direct effect by raising the demand for, therefore the price of, food; and the swelling incomes of farmers and the rents of landlords thus created a reserve of spending power in the property-owning and entrepreneurial sectors of society. In the period 1650 to 1750, however, population growth took place without the corresponding rise in prices. On the contrary it was accompanied by a fall, and therefore must have tended to create increasing purchasing power in the hands of the masses of the people who were enabled to buy the products of industry owing to the increasing margin of income over subsistence; and since (after the upward trend of population declared itself again in the 1740s) there were more people buying industrial goods *per capita*, the total volume of consumption must have risen substantially. A foundation for mass consumption was being laid by the inverse developments of population and progressive agriculture.

Related to this movement of price–population variables is a further characteristic of great interest, namely, that each of the upward phases of the pattern of population and prices appears to be associated with a notable expansion of the economy in aggregate output. The medieval boom in population was associated with one of the greatest building booms in the nation's history. The thirteenth-century renaissance, marked by an efflorescence of ecclesiastical and military architecture, was founded on an overwhelming labour supply which flooded the towns and villages and even desert places, as the history of medieval colonization abundantly shows. Profits poured into the laps of rural entrepreneurs, lay and ecclesiastical, from rising rents, rising entry fines, rising prices, but falling real wages. There was a profit inflation at the expense of wage labour and pressure on agricultural resources to the point at which there was a severe cut-back of agricultural productivity through soil deterioration and falling yields.

It was not merely that agricultural techniques were unable to respond to the challenge of increased demand; it was worse than this. The techniques that had sufficed to enable the population to reach the existing limit began to recede owing to the encroachment of arable upon the pasture in order to provide the basic necessity of bread at the expense of the more expendable commodity of meat; and the development of industry and trade was not such as to provide compensation in terms of added employment for the land shortage in agriculture. The cloth industry, which one might have thought should have fulfilled this role 'could not expand its sales at the rate of population increase; even its lower quality branches suffered from stagnant purchasing power as the real incomes of the majority failed to rise, and the only market of any buoyancy was among the top levels of the peasantry' (Pollard and Crossley, p. 82). Every condition of a Malthusian crisis appeared to be present here, in the thirteenth century. It is important to note them, as it is doubtful if another example of this magnitude or duration can be cited for the entire range of English history. It is possible to argue—but hardly to prove—that the Malthusian problem was solved once and for all from 1348 by biological agencies of which bubonic plague was one, resulting in a reduction of population but a stimulus to agrarian organization which banished the Malthusian threat as a menace to the national life, apart from local crises. At the same time, such conditions made for new growth which could take advantage of the favourable equilibrium between numbers and resources. In other words, the period of stagnation or even retreat that followed had its advantages as well as disadvantages from the point of view of growth of resources. The shortage of labour caused the wages of unskilled labourers to rise and encouraged them to make themselves independent by taking on land; poor land was converted to sheep pasture; arable was less overcropped and yields showed signs of rising. Even the deserted villages may sometimes be regarded as examples not of decay, but of the substitution for poor, cold land of better sites by surviving tenants, though those dating from 1450, when population was beginning to recover, were undertaken for other motives and often involved depopulation. But one novel characteristic imported into the agricultural economy had permanent significance; owners began to go out of their way to attract tenants by repairing farmhouses or by including in their leases undertakings to maintain farm buildings. The specifically English system of landlord–tenant relationships which played such an important part in the advance of agriculture was coming into being.

The period also saw the laying of the foundation of the English cloth industry in spite of the rise in labour costs. Apart from the advantages the industry enjoyed through the supply of home-grown wool and the fiscal devices adopted by government to deny them to the foreign competitors, it also enjoyed a widening home market. Labourers who were beginning to get themselves a holding and yeomen who were rising into the ranks of the gentry could turn their attention to personal wants, and labour shortage encouraged the spread of the fulling mill, especially in the forest areas where labour power and water power could be brought together for industrial production. In the iron industry the effects of labour shortage were felt more directly. There was a major increase in the use of water-power which so lowered costs and prices of the product of the improved bloomeries that 'total output might well have increased around 1400, at a time when the agricultural demand for iron would be rising with the increase in wealthier peasants' surplus for improvements' (Pollard and Crossley, p. 75).

On the other hand, certain adverse effects of the fall in population must also be mentioned. Where economic life was centred entirely on agriculture there was necessarily less activity of internal trade than before, and Professor Everitt has pointed to a drastic reduction in the size of some market towns and in the total number of markets. A survey in the seventeenth century revealed that there were fewer market towns than there had been three centuries earlier. 'Scores and hundreds of markets had perished in the generations following the Black Death and were never revived.' In Norfolk, where at one time there had been 130, there were now [in 1640] only 31. The 53 that had existed in Gloucestershire were now down to 34; and of the 85 markets and fairs in Lancashire that had received charters, and 50 that had them by prescription, there were in 1640 no more than 30 markets in the whole county (Thirsk, 1967, p. 469). The complaint of the decay of towns which has given the period a dismal reputation of economic retreat thus had a substantial foundation, but set alongside the evidence of growth—of the cloth trade, the agriculture of the thriving yeomanry and peasants, the improvement in the iron trade, and the prosperity of cloth merchants dealing in foreign trade on the secure base of an expanding home market—it is difficult to strike an adverse balance. To quote the authors to whom this account owes so much, total wealth 'may well have declined', but 'wealth *per capita* certainly rose and in rising, acquired a more even spread'. Again, both in agriculture and in industry, 'this period and the fifteenth century in particular, provided a breathing space which allowed natural resources to develop to meet the needs of a new century of rising population and expanding foreign markets' (Pollard and Crossley, p. 82). This language may well be recalled when we come to describe the effects of the demographic lull before the great breakthrough in the second half of the eighteenth century.

The period of demographic expansion that followed the lull of the fifteenth century was accompanied by the now familiar signs of enlargement of aggregate national resources, side by side with falling *per capita* income under the pressure of increasing numbers on the relatively inelastic output of agriculture. It will be remembered that a few years ago we used to speak of the 'Industrial Revolution of 1550–1650' as a result of Professor Nef's enthusiastic account of the growth in the production of coal, iron, glass, salt, in Elizabethan times. Professor W. G. Hoskins (1953) has told the story of the rebuilding of England when the houses of yeomen, gentlemen, and nobility sprang up in villages and towns left us with a gracious heritage that neither modern taxation nor even modern town planning can entirely extirpate. We should remember too that the price revolution of the sixteenth century, which used to be fathered on the import of bullion to Spanish ports, is now firmly placed on the doorstep of a demographic boom; Professor Phelps-Brown has shown that increasing population raised the demand for agricultural products, in particular corn (p. 299), which floated English farmers and landlords on a tide of prosperity and opened to them opportunities for agrarian innovation of which the best of them began to take advantage. They were especially stimulated by the growth of London where the pressure of the market was advancing at an astounding pace. There was a condition of favourable terms of trade between country and town which led to a great outflow of capital to the countryside. It was also a period of colonial expansion which was partly aimed at finding outlets for surplus population. As Sir Humphrey Gilbert (himself a founder of colonies) said, 'England is pestered with people', for which his contemporary Hakluyt found a reason: owing to our 'seldome sickness' (Coleman, 1956, p. 293). The basis of the trading area which was to play such an important part as a leading sector in the eighteenth century was being laid.

Dr Wrigley, however, takes the view that population growth was too fast and brought its own Malthusian nemesis in its train. 'One of the reasons', he writes,

why the industrial revolution of the sixteenth century which Nef has documented had no chance of fructifying into a steady expansion in production and real incomes was that population behaved much in the way Malthus supposed to be almost inevitable. The sixteenth century English economy and population was 'over-fishing' and paid the penalty, just as the Irish population of the late eighteenth and early nineteenth century was 'over-fishing' (1966, p. 107).

While not explicitly controverting this verdict, the studiously moderate scholarly summary of Pollard and Crossley hardly confirms this view. 'It is hard to escape the conclusion', they write,

that increases [in prices] were due in large measure to the failure of production to keep pace with a rising demand largely brought about by a rise in population . . . all that sixteenth-century agriculture seems to have achieved was the avoidance of a spiral of soil exhaustion and falling yields which could have led to a catastrophic decline in lower-class living standards, comparable with the late thirteenth century.

While a Malthusian crisis on the thirteenth-century scale had been avoided on the side of food supply, they find clear evidence that 'growing population was leading to a measure of rising production and an expansion in trade', especially in internal trade where the radius of the London market was creeping out along the rivers and sea routes, and where middlemen were penetrating ever more deeply into the countryside to keep the local town markets supplied, and they conclude that 'many more of the changes in the economy may be traced back, directly or indirectly, to the population factor, which was of just such an extent to encourage enterprise but not to create those conditions of miserable poverty seen three centuries before' (pp. 95, 113, 124).

The bottle-neck of inadequate transport that tended to block the transport of goods from areas of surplus to areas of shortage and so prevent the opening up of the prospect of steady expansion in production and real income remained unbroken, but it is at least as feasible to argue that the responsibility lay with the check to demand that followed the new wave of epidemic disease as to attribute it to population pressure which had reached its peak by the beginning of the new century. Within the next decade, farmers and landlords were beginning to feel the pinch of plenty which may well be associated with the succession of epidemics, particularly of plague, that gathered force in the last years of the sixteenth century and culminated in a savage attack in 1625 which could scarcely fail to affect the mass demand for food. By this time merchants and farmers were complaining of the fall of prices and this could well be due not only to the increase in supplies flowing from the numerous sources cited by Dr Kerridge, but also to a cutback in demand brought about by the impact of the demographic crisis in the seventeenth century. At what point the rate of growth was sensibly checked it is not easy to say, although the two series of parish figures of which we have record show that the favourable absolute balance of baptisms over burials gave way, *circa* 1640, to a general surplus of burials which lasted for thirty or forty years, or even longer (Wrigley, 1969, pp. 72, 82). In the meantime, the price curve was slackening out and by 1660 was beginning its century-long downward trend.

Professor Stone has drawn our attention to an aspect of the demographic depression to which we shall have to return in a subsequent chapter. He reminds us that it was characterized by a

sharp drop in fertility and a sharp rise in mortality among the upper classes, so that cohorts born between 1625 and 1674 were barely reproducing themselves, and those between 1675 and 1749 were actually falling behind. This dramatic change from the pre-Civil War condition of an excess of children to be accommodated in a relatively static job-market must enormously have reduced social competition . . . after 1660 (pp. 46–7).

It was in fact one of the stabilizing influences that gave the period 1650–1750 a new character of stability and social conservatism so different from the previous century of rampant population growth and social dislocation.

On the economic side, the period was marked by continuous innovation in agriculture which exacerbated the problems of the small farmer who lacked capital to take advantage of it. This, it is suggested, helped to account for the rising problem of poverty, since more and more of the small cultivators were pushed down the scale through competition with their larger and better equipped neighbours. 'When, after about 1640, agriculture began to feel the effects of the end of rising product-prices, problems of poverty became acute . . . while in the sixteenth century [the poor] had been largely the aged and infirm, by 1670 it was not uncommon for half the "exempt" category in Hearth Tax returns to be able-bodied' (Pollard and Crossley, p. 132). But the demographic depression may itself have contributed to this effect since prices, besides being responsive to fluctuating harvests, could also reflect the effect of sudden onsets of disease that cut back the market by reducing the numbers of consumers. Professor Fisher demonstrated this factor in price behaviour in his account of the influenza pandemic of 1558 and there is some evidence that a similar influence was at work during the typhus-and-ague epidemic of the 1680s. A comparison of the Exeter burials and grain prices in the West Country shows a remarkable inverse ratio between prices and burials that suggests the same force at work, i.e. that the high mortalities between 1681 and 1687 were coincidental with low prices and may have themselves exercised a depressing effect by cutting down the size of the consuming market (see Chapter 4).

At the same time, the low level of prices in this decade could not fail to affect the structure of demand among those who enjoyed a surplus over subsistence, for example among the successful farmers who were responding to low prices by improved productivity; merchants who were enjoying the swelling profits of foreign trade and other members of the rising middle classes of whom Stone has given such a vivid account. Moreover, it is recognized that levels of expectation were sensibly rising towards the end of the seventeenth century and leading to rising standards of living in all social classes that had the means to aspire to it. This tendency enhances the importance of the next phase of population growth, the sharp rise that I have indicated in the period 1690–1720. Hypothetical as this may be regarded in the light of our present knowledge, the evidence for it, in my view, is sufficiently impressive to call for attention. If I am right, it would seem that side by side with the commercial boom in foreign trade, there were also forces at work to stimulate a new phase in the home market: a series of bad harvests—the 'seven ill years' of the 1690s—brought high prices and prosperity to farmers and landlords, and secondly, a weakening of the epidemic cycle which resulted in a fall in the level of mortalities, a balance of births over deaths, and a substantial rise in the total population.

In explanation of this paradoxical situation I would like to quote the account I gave on a former occasion, which, after ten years of reconsideration, I see no reason to change:

To go back to the 1690's, the period of the notorious seven 'ill years' (1692-9) which caused such havoc in Scotland, we find that the response of the English provincial towns and villages was less marked than might have been expected. Even London failed to provide the evidence of demographic decline appropriate to a period of high prices and social distress. There was no unusual sickness, except in 1694 and the year 1696 when the mean price of wheat reached 56s. had 'the smallest number of deaths from all causes since many years before'. The effect was stated by Dr Short to be chiefly felt in the country at large, but as Dr Creighton says, 'when we look for the evidence of this in England we shall have difficulty in finding it'. Though scattered references in different parts of the country suggest that the seven ill years were not without their depressing effects on population growth, Dr Short's own abstracts give almost no colour to it. As far as the data of this inquiry go, they show a rise in burials—by no means spectacular—between 1692 and 1695 and a fall in baptisms followed by a reversal of these trends and a substantial balance of baptisms over burials which is maintained for a period of twenty-two years' (Chambers, 1957, p. 28).

How far these conditions were associated with the remarkable economic activities of the period it is impossible to say with any precision. But that such a relationship existed can hardly be doubted. Professor John has noted that the fall in bread-grain prices in the 1680s was marked and that the long-term fall in the south-eastern and parts of south-western England was sufficient to release purchasing power for manufactures (1967, p. 191). If this was followed by a rise in the population, the conditions were favourable for a general advance, and evidence of such an advance is not far to seek in a period that includes the launching of numerous navigation schemes assisted by the introduction of the pound lock; the initiation of turnpikes, branching out from London; a development of textiles that included framework knitting in the East Midlands, silk-weaving and fustian manufacture and ribbon-weaving in the West Midlands and Lancashire; the remarkable silk mills at Derby; the growth of pottery and hardware in Staffordshire and the West Midlands; and the revolutionary innovations of Abraham Darby and Thomas Newcomen.

The limiting factors of this promising advance are discussed elsewhere (see Chapter 6), but nature itself played a crucial part by descending with the last of her compensatory prunings which put a temporary stop to population growth through the renewal of the epidemic cycle, marked by mortality peaks in 1719, 1727–9, 1736, 1740–1. Perhaps the check to population growth that was given in 1720–40 had a role to play, as it had in the fifteenth century, by making possible a substantial rise in the living conditions of the labour force and by introducing a rudimentary conception of a rising standard of living which they could make an effort to maintain when numbers began to rise in the next decade to challenge it. The 'critical mass' to use Professor Landes's expression, a piling up of various factors favouring England's growth (Hartwell, p. 173), was receiving the kind of stimulus that the demographic factor was able to give in the special circumstances of England's economic evolution.

2
Marriage and Mobility as Factors in Pre-Industrial Development in England

---

THE relevance of such familiar topics as marriage and mobility to pre-industrial economic development may not be immediately obvious, but in view of the activity that is taking place in the field of demographic studies there is evidently a case for their re-examination. In a recent article, Mr Clay makes a powerful case for the revision of the part played by marriage in the concentration of landownership in England in the eighteenth century in the light of Hollingsworth's study of the British aristocracy and their strange inability to provide an adequate succession of male heirs in the period 1650–1720; and to go further afield both in space and time, we have recently been told by Professor Herlihy of the close relationship that existed between the fluctuations in the fertility of the peasants of Pistoia in fourteenth-century Italy and the economic well-being of that region. Clearly demographic studies, as an aid to historical interpretation, have arrived, and it is hoped that an elementary summary of the findings in this branch of the subject as it affects our understanding of English historical development may not be out of place.

The subject of this chapter—marriage and its correlative, movement in search of a job, a house, and a partner in life—obviously has close affinities with the factors of economic change. In Western societies, marriage was the passport to the establishment of an independent family unit, and the family, in its economic aspect, was a microcosm of the society of which it was part, a form of economy in which the administration of scarce means was a matter of everyday concern and frequently of anxiety to the head of it. Its head was unquestionably exercising the arts of the acquisitive society without consciously invoking the Protestant ethic.

In an underdeveloped economy, the average family lives near the margin of subsistence. If the family thrives, the nation thrives, and if we can find out how the average family thrives we are in a fair way to knowing the roots of the progress of the economy as a whole. This is all the more important in view of the fact that the structure of the family in Western Europe, the original home of industrialism, is now thought to be unique. Such a view was presented a few years ago in an important paper by Professor Hajnal, although it was anticipated in a number of important respects in that classic of demographic studies, *Culture and Human Fertility*, edited by Professor Lorimer.

THE 'WESTERN EUROPEAN' MARRIAGE PATTERN

Hajnal finds that a marked difference can be shown to have existed east and west of a line drawn roughly between Leningrad and Trieste (pp. 101–2). East of the line families were larger, and celibacy was rare, whilst marriages were more numerous and took place at an earlier age; on the other hand, relatively late marriage as the prelude to the establishment of an independent family unit, together with a high incidence of celibacy, at least among the propertied classes, appears to have been the norm for the greater part of the society of Western Europe, in contrast with the patriarchal or extended family associated with early marriage and high nuptiality elsewhere. Hajnal is so impressed by this that he is prepared to present it as an underlying factor in the differential economic development of the two regions. The marriage pattern of Western Europe, was, he says, unique, as was the economic development. Is this uniqueness in demographic and economic development purely coincidental? He points out that the lateness of marriage in Western society would provide a longer period during which couples would save and make provision for marriage. It would raise demand for goods other than food, and the total demand in a society of this kind, he argues, would be much greater than in one in which a small class of wealthy families was superimposed on a mass population living at subsistence level. 'Could this effect,' he asks, 'which was uniquely European, help to explain how the ground-work was laid for the uniquely European "take-off" into modern economic growth?' (p. 132). We are thus confronted with the hypothesis that Western society was equipped with a built-in device for differential development through the pattern of marriage and structure of the family, and in particular through the relatively high age at which marriage took place.

Some degree of confirmation of this hypothesis may be drawn from the results of an inquiry by Professor Hoselitz on the subject of population pressure and industrialization in underdeveloped countries. He observes (pp. 123–5), 'There are significant differences in the conditions which existed when Europe industrialized and those we find in Asia today. . . . One of the most obvious is the much greater rural density of population in most Asian countries', which, he says, 'whether measured in terms of occupied males or in terms of households, [is] roughly three or more times as high in present day underdeveloped countries in Asia, than in Europe at a corresponding period of the economic development of these countries.' Since there exists (on the basis of studies by Professor Colin Clark) 'a rather high correlation between agricultural land per agricultural worker and average output per head of population' the part played by the unique character of the marriage pattern of the region of early industrialization becomes a matter of some importance in considering the different tempo of its economic development.

It is the object of this chapter to explore a little further than has yet been done the part played by the West European marriage pattern in creating conditions that could have led to the differential rate of growth in the area in which it obtains. But it should first be emphasized that the argument of economic differentiation arising out of the contrasting family structures does not rely exclusively on the higher fertility of the one with its attendant increase of pressure on economic resources, compared to the other. Certainly, such a demographic differential did exist: as Lorimer says (p. 180), 'the fertility of Asiatic agrarian societies has always been *incongruous* with their ecological situation. It tended to induce a rate of increase of these populations that could not be supported by the economic basis of their existence.' At the same time, however, he cites figures to show that fertility in some areas of the extended family could be as low or lower than in Western Europe and cites many reasons from local social and cultural conditions that could account for it. The difference between the two types was, therefore, cultural as well as demographic. Whereas the independent family of the West had to stand on its own feet and was expected to have an adequate financial basis before marriage was entered into, the co-operative groups of the areas of the extended family, although without 'an intrinsic tendency to provide strong motives for high fertility', nevertheless supported their members in bearing and nurturing children, and gave them, therefore, a sense of security on venturing into marriage and parenthood (Lorimer, pp. 200–1). No such thing could be said with respect to Western marriage. Here is the essential difference between the two societies, and by underlining the unique character of the Western structure of the family, Hajnal has indicated the direction in which we should look for its distinctive characteristics on the economic side, i.e. the pursuit of economic advantage as the criterion of individual and collective effort.

The first consideration to which we should address ourselves is to try to determine approximately the period when the European marriage pattern emerged and the factors, ideological and material, that influenced its development. Hajnal himself is in some doubt about this. He advances the opinion, somewhat tentatively, that 'some change in marriage habits took place between the fourteenth century and the eighteenth', and adds that 'it does not seem possible that the populations of medieval Europe had the fully developed European pattern' (p. 120); that is, the two-generation pattern with few or no in-law members under the same roof as distinct from the non-European patriarchal family of several generations living as an amorphous group of blood relations.

Only the literary historians appear to have given much thought to this question. They find that the subject of marriage is at the core of the literary imagination from the end of the seventeenth to the beginning of the nineteenth century, and attribute it to a revolution that is alleged to have taken place in the late seventeenth century in the history of marriage. It took the form, says Professor Watt (pp. 138–9), following the model of the French sociologist Durkheim, of a transition from the patriarchal large family held together by ties of kin to the independent, nuclear, or, in Durkheim's phrase, the conjugal family: 'an entity formed by the voluntary union of two persons'. Such a family would be established immediately on marriage, often far away from the parents, as an 'autonomous unit' in economic and social affairs. It was associated, he suggests, with the growth of individualism and with the Puritan attitude to marriage as a God-given union and was essentially new.

That there is an important suggestion here for the economic historian who is concerned with the phenomenon of business enterprise in England of the seventeenth and eighteenth centuries is obvious. Does the emergence of the conjugal family help to explain the fever or entrepreneurial activity with which economic historians are so familiar? Its association with the Puritan view of marriage as the life-long union of two persons dedicated by mutual vows to the creation and support of a family and drawing none of its sanctity from the sacramental blessing of the Church fits in well with the currently accepted ethos of pre-industrial enterprise; and the paradox of prudential nuptiality which is also the expression of romantic love has many authentic exemplars in the records which business historians have brought to light.

The demographic historian, however, would wish to make a number of qualifications to this view. To begin with, it is especially difficult to follow Watt when he says that 'the term family, in Gregory King, as in Shakespeare, refers to a whole household and often includes grand-parents, cousins and even remoter kin, as well as servants and other employees. . . . In the seventeenth century the traditional and patriarchal family pattern was by far the commonest' (p. 140). A glance at Gregory King's calculation of the social structure of England in 1688 (Table 2) shows, in fact, that the very large household pertained only to the social classes from the level of the gentry upwards, a small fraction of the total. Below the gentry came a range of social categories with an average of 5–8 per household; and below these in turn came the vast mass of the population with families ranging in size from 5 for the farmers to $3\frac{1}{4}$ for cottagers and paupers. The poorest families, it will be noticed, were the smallest. Many examples from the study of individual villages could be cited in confirmation of this general picture of family size. In his study of Kent (pp. 35–8), Dr Chalklin finds that large families of over 5 children were rare; among approximately 270 households in the parish of Ash-next-Sandwich in 1705 there were 522 children, or an average of a little under 2 each; only 10 families had more than 5 children and none had more than 8. Moreover, he finds that those of the labourers were the smallest of all; where the tradesmen and farmers had about $2\frac{1}{2}$ children on the average, the labourer had little over $1\frac{1}{2}$. It should be remembered, of course, that these were not necessarily completed families, and that older children from the age of twelve

TABLE 2

Tables of Estimates by Gregory King, Charles Davenant, and W. Couling

A Scheme of the Income and Expense of the several Families of England, calculated for the year 1688.[1]

Number of Families	Ranks, Degrees, Titles, and Qualifications	Heads per Family	Number of Persons	Yearly Income per Family £ s.	Yearly Income in General £	Yearly Income per Head £ s.	Yearly Expense per Head £ s. d.	Yearly Increase per Head £ s. d.	Yearly Increase in General £
160	Temporal lords	40	6,400	3,200 0	512,000	80 0	70 0 0	10 0 0	64,000
26	Spiritual lords	20	520	1,300 0	33,800	65 0	45 0 0	20 0 0	10,400
800	Baronets	16	12,800	880 0	704,000	55 0	49 0 0	6 0 0	76,800
600	Knights	13	7,800	650 0	390,000	50 0	45 0 0	5 0 0	39,000
3,000	Esquires	10	30,000	450 0	1,200,000	45 0	41 0 0	4 0 0	120,000
12,000	Gentlemen	8	96,000	280 0	2,880,000	35 0	32 0 0	3 0 0	288,000
5,000	Persons in greater offices and places	8	40,000	240 0	1,200,000	30 0	26 0 0	4 0 0	160,000
5,000	Persons in lesser offices and places	6	30,000	120 0	600,000	20 0	17 0 0	3 0 0	90,000
2,000	Eminent merchants and traders by sea	8	16,000	400 0	800,000	50 0	37 0 0	13 0 0	208,000
8,000	Lesser merchants and traders by sea	6	48,000	198 0	1,600,000	53 0	27 0 0	6 0 0	288,000
10,000	Persons in the law	7	70,000	154 0	1,540,000	22 0	13 0 0	4 0 0	280,000
2,000	Eminent clergymen	6	12,000	72 0	144,000	12 0	10 0 0	2 0 0	24,000
8,000	Lesser clergymen	5	40,000	50 0	400,000	10 0	9 4 0	0 16 0	32,000
40,000	Freeholders of the better sort	7	280,000	91 0	3,640,000	13 0	11 15 0	1 5 0	350,000
120,000	Freeholders of the lesser sort[2]	5½	660,000	55 0	6,600,000	10 0	9 10 0	0 10 0	330,000
150,000	Farmers	5	750,000	42 10	6,375,000	8 10	3 5 0	0 5 0	187,500

15,000	Persons in liberal arts and sciences	5	75,000	60 0	900,000	12 0	11 0 0	1 0 0	75,000
50,000	Shopkeepers and tradesmen	4½	225,000	45 0	2,250,000	10 0	9 0 0	1 0 0	225,000
60,000	Artisans and handicrafts	4	240,000	38 0	2,280,000	9 10	9 0 0	0 10 0	120,000
5,000	Naval officers	4	20,000	80 0	400,000	20 0	18 0 0	2 0 0	40,000
4,000	Military officers	4	16,000	60 0	240,000	15 0	14 0 0	1 0 0	16,000
500,586		5⅓	2,675,520	68 18	34,488,800	12 18	11 15 4	1 2 8	3,023,700
								Decrease	Decrease
50,000	Common seamen	3	150,000	20 0	1,000,000	7 0	7 10 0	0 10 0	75,000
364,000	Labouring people and out-servants	3½	1,275,000	15 0	5,460,000	4 10	4 12 0	0 2 0	127,500
400,000	Cottagers and paupers	3¼	1,300,000	6 10	2,000,000	2 0	2 5 0	0 5 0	325,000
35,000	Common soldiers	2	70,000	14 0	490,000	7 0	7 10 0	0 10 0	35,000
849,000		3¼	2,795,000	10 10	8,950,000	3 5	3 9 0	0 4 0	562,500
	Vagrants; as gipsies, thieves, beggars, etc.		30,000		60,000	2 0	4 0 0	2 0 0	60,000

So the general account is

500,586	Increasing the wealth of the kingdom	5⅓	2,675,520	68 18	34,488,800	12 18	11 15 4	1 2 8	3,023,700
849,000	Decreasing the wealth of the kingdom	3¼	2,825,000	10 10	9,010,000	3 3	3 7 6	0 4 6	622,500
1,349,586	Net totals	4 1/13	5,500,520	32 5	43,491,800	7 18	7 9 3	0 8 9	2,401,200

[1] *Political and Commercial Works of Charles Davenant*, collected and revised by Sir C. Whitworth, vol. ii, p. 184 (London, 1761).
[2] Gregory King gives 140,000 as the number of 'lesser' freeholders.

or fifteen would probably be out at service in the larger households in their own or neighbouring parishes; but even including servants, the mean number per household in the three boroughs in the parish of Sevenoaks, was only 4·3.

Much more evidence of the same kind could be cited, and Mr Laslett's summary of this aspect of seventeenth-century family structure is not likely to be challenged. After examining numerous examples of family size in the seventeenth century he concludes:

> In all the communities for which evidence has so far been recovered, the presence of children living at home after marriage was even rarer than the presence of parents living with married children . . . living with in-laws can only have been occasionally. . . . It is impossble that it can have been the ordinary, expected thing to do (p. 91).

He goes on to show that it was considerably less common than it is today.

In other words, the small independent family unit was already the rule for the great bulk of the population. The attempt by sociologists and the literary historians who follow them to father the European family unit on the influence of Puritan individualism cannot stand the test of demographic analysis and must be abandoned. It has its roots much deeper both in time and historical circumstances. Professor Raftis, for instance, in his study of *Tenure and Mobility* (p. 209), finds it back in the fifteenth century; 'it is the small modern family—man, wife and children—that appears uniquely in the village documents in the fifteenth century'. When the remnants of the village demesnes were finally farmed out in the fifteenth century they passed in all instances to one or two men rather than to a group of villagers. Professor Hallam, writing of the villages of the silt-lands of Lincolnshire in the thirteenth century, is even more emphatic and precise. Even in the villages practising the archaic system of partible inheritance, the inhabitants lived in separate households. Occasionally three generations did live together—5·6 per cent of households in one village, 1·6 per cent in another, while in a third there were none. In only one household was there a middle-aged spinster or bachelor living with a married brother (1958, p. 332).

Now that the classical historians are turning their attention to the demographic aspect of their studies, there is some possibility that the elusive problem of the origin of the European small family unit may be traced to its source. Suggestive advances have been made in two directions; in an unpublished study of the Roman army, Dr Watson has traced the change in the Roman marriage laws which aimed at enabling the soldiers on garrison duty on the frontier to establish stable family units so as to leave their property to legitimate offspring. By the third or fourth century, he observes that the soldiers on garrison duty on the frontier could be said to be living in married quarters; and since the soldier himself was separated from his family of origin it would seem to follow that the independent family unit, as we understand it, had made its appearance as an incidental result of the effort by the Imperial authorities to provide a stream of recruits from the soldiers themselves.

Another promising line of inquiry has been opened up by a study of the epigraphic evidence from memorial stones which provide data regarding the age of marriage in the late Roman Empire. In a recent article on this subject Mr M. K. Hopkins draws attention to the remarkably early age at which girls married in the late Roman Empire, and notes that though the legal minimum age for girls to marry in the time of Augustus was 12, consummated marriages not infrequently took place earlier, and he cites the example of Octavia, daughter of the Emperor Claudius, who was married at 11. Other examples of early marriage in high places are those of Agrippina, married to Nero at 12; while the wife of Tacitus the historian was hardly more than 13. More significant for our present purpose, however, is his finding that there was a tendency for the age at marriage to rise with the spread of Christianity. His conclusions may be summarized as follows: the modal age at marriage of pagan girls was 12 to 15; that of Christian girls from 15 to 18. The average age of Christian girls marrying before 25 was 16·82 contrasted with 15·5 of pagan girls, while the average age of Christian men at marriage was 27 compared with 26 for pagan men. He concludes that 'there seems to have been a rise in the age of marriage in Christian times' and thinks that the change could be regarded 'as in some way a by-product of Christian asceticism; . . . [but] it is still necessary to explain what pressures drove Christians to delay marriage in the cause of asceticism' (pp. 313, 316–17, 319–20, 325–6).

Whatever doubts there may be about the effect of Christian influence upon the age at marriage, in regard to another aspect of equal importance, namely the stability of marriage as affected by divorce, there can be no doubt; its influence may be described as revolutionary. Under the influence of the Church the loose and unstable form of marriage that prevailed in the Roman world was gradually transformed into a sacramental contract, fully recognized by the twelfth century. Marriages without ecclesiastical benediction did occur of course, and were generally thought to be valid; but in 1563 the Council of Trent directed that henceforth no marriage could be recognized without a religious ceremony (Westermarck, pp. 427–8).

Moreover, the Church was exercising its influence in extending the marriage institution down the social scale. In the Middle Ages the serf and all he possessed, not excluding his offspring and the progeny of his horses and cattle (together designated as *sequela*), were ultimately, in legal theory, the property of his lord (Bennet, p. 240). Yet by the twelfth century the Church ventured to declare the binding force of marriage between two serfs even against the will of their lord or lords, and in the thirteenth came out for the serf's right to make a will (Bennet, p. 249).

Other secular factors, such as the growth of a class of freemen and influences connected with landholding and inheritance (particularly primogeniture), worked to a similiar effect. Manorial custom allowed both free and unfree tenants to pass on the tenancy to a son; and Professor Homans has shown that in Medieval England marriage was associated essentially with the acquisition or the sharing or a holding which could provide the elements of subsistence for a family. 'No land no marriage' was the rule unless the landless man could marry an heiress—usually a widow—or migrate to the town and get himself accepted as an apprentice to a trade, which would in any case forbid his marrying until he reached a relatively advanced age (Chapters XI–XII).

The question of which of these various influences was paramount or anterior to the other is not under discussion; but it is worth noting that the influence of the Church was to fix the marriage structure into an immovable mould, and it is a familiar phenomenon of demographic history that once a custom has been established it tends to outlive the circumstances that called it into being and to continue a life of its own.

This is especially true in regard to one aspect of the pre-industrial marriage structure in which the ideological factor reinforced the secular interests of the post-medieval village community with potentially important effects on fertility. I refer to the campaign waged unremittingly by the Church and parochial authorities against bastardy and to a lesser extent against pre-marital pregnancy, again in the name of Christian asceticism. This campaign was carried out through the medium of the ecclesiastical courts which were empowered to exercise a jurisdiction over the entire range of behaviour that lay outside the actual limits of the civil and criminal law, and over a very wide spectrum of the social hierarchy, including the clergy themselves and even occasionally the gentry. The records of these courts show that the control vested in the clergy over the morals of the rank and file of the parish were vigilantly exercised in many, perhaps in most, parishes with some degree of success. When a culprit confessed or was found guilty of a moral offence, he was enjoined to perform a penance or make 'compurgation', i.e. a swearing by his neighbours on his behalf; and if the church wardens failed to make a presentment an interested party could promote a case on his account. The object of these prosecutions, it was laid down, was that all who behaved

wantonly, wickedly, or unchastlie, or unseemly are by the law cannons and constitutions customs and government of the Church of England to be censured and afterwards corrected and punished by the Ecclesiastical Judge to the end that others of them by their punishment and correction may be terrified and affrighted from committing the like offence and scandal and live godly righteous virtuous and chaste lives in all godliness and honesty.

At almost every session of the court there were sinners in the flesh and persons 'lying under common fame of being so'; and a couple that produced a child within nine months of the marriage could scarcely hope to escape censure, sometimes the refusal of the Communion cup.

Among the duties of the court was the licensing of midwives. They were chosen for their good character as well as for their skill. They had to swear not to do any sorcery or incantation, and could demand the ringing of the church bell in a difficult labour or the tying of an old piece of bell-rope round the woman's waist. But of greater importance to the demographer was the oath that they had to take to exhort the mothers of bastard children to give the names of the fathers; and when this practice fell into decay in the early eighteenth century, there were complaints that

the fathers of illegitimate children had thereby escaped detection
and the parishes had had to assume their burden. The maintenance
of an ecclesiastical penitential system would make the concealment
of a bastard a relatively difficult matter, at least in lowland
England's close-knit village communities, a fact that gives added
credence to the statistics of illegitimacy collected by demographers.

Although, in this respect, there were wide variations from 1 per
cent of baptisms in many parishes to 10 per cent in others, there
is a consensus of opinion that from roughly the Elizabethan to the
Georgian age, the proportion of recorded illegitimate births was
surprisingly low, not more than 5 per cent, though it rose substantially after 1750 (Glass and Eversley, p. 51); and further, that
pregnancy was by no means a pre-condition of marriage. In fact,
there is some evidence of trial marriage in the evidence brought in
the Consistory Courts in Elizabethan times, which implies pre-
marital sexual relations since a promise to marry given before
witnesses—usually the parents—and the exchange of presents, such
as a pair of gloves, was regarded as a free contract. In the light of
such practices, one might imagine that the low level of bastardy
should have been balanced by a high level of pre-marital conceptions; these however do not seem to have been much above
10 per cent in the seventeeth-century Midlands and Home Counties,
although they rose to 40 per cent in some areas by the end of the
eighteenth century (see Chapter 3). Since the incidence of bastardy
was still lower—indeed far lower—in France where clerical influence was especially strong, we may conclude that the disciplinary
efforts of the Church courts were an active factor in restraining
fertility in pre-industrial England, and that pre-marital sexual
behaviour was under greater control than might have been
expected, especially in view of the relatively late age of marriage.

MARRIAGE AND MOBILITY: THE AGE AT MARRIAGE IN
ENGLAND

It has usually been assumed that obstacles to mobility such as
limitations of transport and particularly the operation of the
Settlement Laws must have imposed limitations upon the choice
of partners and served to keep down the rate of marriage. While
these factors cannot be dismissed altogether, they must be relegated
to secondary importance in the light of the mounting evidence
that neither the Settlement Laws nor the condition of transport

constituted a serious barrier to the movement of single able-bodied young men and women—as distinct from heads of families—in search of a job, a house, or a partner in life. Moreover, this remarkable fluidity of the labour force was of great antiquity. Professor Hallam finds that in the thirteenth-century Lincolnshire villages he examined, the proportion lost by migration was remarkably high, especially in those communities in which opportunities for permanent settlement were reduced by primogeniture; and in the fifteenth century we are told that manor competed with manor for labour and tenants (Raftis, p. 172). Usually migration took place over a radius of 15 or 20 miles; but there are examples of men and women from Ramsey in Huntingdonshire getting as far as Lincoln and Dr Ekwall has pointed out that London received sufficient immigrants to create the Midland English that Chaucer spoke. From the number of Midland words in the language of London, he concludes that Midlanders formed the literate élite of the metropolis (pp. xi–xiv). In fact, the mobility of village folk in the fifteenth century seems to have anticipated that of the eighteenth and it is fair to say that the pattern of inter-village exchange of population of Huntingdonshire in the eighteenth century could be superimposed upon that of the manors of Ramsey Abbey in the fifteenth without substantial adjustment.

The evidence for mobility in later centuries is still more convincing. A study of village names in the Subsidy Rolls of Nottinghamshire villages between 1606 and 1641 shows that although the population had not altered appreciably in size between the two dates, more than 37 per cent of the names vanished, and their place was taken by others. 'Names continually disappear,' the author writes, 'while new names occur, themselves in turn vanishing, leaving finally perhaps one family running through the series for a parish.' Whatever the cause, these figures indicate a greater change than any due to the ordinary chances of life. 'It seems therefore permissible to infer that the rural population . . . was not permanently rooted in its native soil' (Peyton, pp. 248–50). These findings have been confirmed by more recent studies, and the picture of a mobile country population incessantly engaged in the process of moving for the purpose of improving their condition, above all seeking their fortune in the towns, is now firmly established.

An important recent contribution to our knowledge of this

phenomenon is that provided by Dr Tranter, who was fortunate enough to come across a detailed survey of Cardington in Bedfordshire for the year 1782. In the single year of the survey 5 out of 150 cottage families moved out of the village, which, if it is a representative figure, could mean that the entire cottage population would change in thirty years. Of those who reached the age of fifteen, 64 per cent of the boys and 57 per cent of the girls had left the parish to earn a living elsewhere, usually as domestic servants or in husbandry. Half the cottage migrants went to villages within an approximate distance of 6 miles; only 27 per cent went beyond the boundary of the county and most of these went to London. The inward flow into the village was on almost a similar scale: of the 109 families whose places of birth were given, only 7 had both parents born in it: 51 had both parents from another parish; of the men 33 per cent and of the women 27 per cent were born in the village. There was a stable element of propertied families with roots in the village and it seems to have been from them that the tradition of a static rural society had its rise and justification (1966, pp. 297–303; 1967, pp. 276–7).

From this, and many other inquiries which could be cited, it would appear that the limit of settlement was not the parish, but a larger area comprising several parishes covering a distance of about 7 miles across. Apparently the pre-industrial villager knew the neighbouring parishes as intimately as he knew his own; when a cottage became vacant it would be snapped up as readily by a man from the next village as by those in the village where it occurred. Boys and girls would not only leave home, but leave their native parishes for places in service, and also for their partners in marriage. Moreover the high death-rate and low expectation of life would provide opportunities which these humble seekers after self-advancement would not let slip. Perhaps the most striking and poignant example of the incessant movement of the labouring classes in search of a living comes from the parish of Wrangle in Lincolnshire, where the ravages of tuberculosis and ague arising from the proximity of undrained fenland were so severe that the average life-span of all children born there in 1654–1753 was merely fourteen. Yet in spite of this appalling wastage of life, the village maintained itself at a steady level of between 200 and 300 owing to the inward movement of migrants from neighbouring villages in search of a livelihood, a cottage, or a partner in marriage.

Some of the most convincing evidence of the fluidity of the marriage market comes from regional studies of marriage registers. Mr Skipp, in his interesting study of Bickenhill, found that in the seventy years before the passing of Lord Hardwicke's Marriage Act of 1753 no less than 213 marriages took place between strangers to the parishes—but not one after this act; and during the same period the proportion of marriages in which one partner was drawn from another parish usually reached about 50 per cent (pp. 39–40). Moreover, when we consider the wide dispersal of the partners in clandestine marriages, it is difficult to think that the course of true love was easily diverted by such feeble considerations as the distance that separated the lovers. In the little village of Fledborough in Nottinghamshire, where between 1712 and 1730 only eleven marriages were solemnized, the grant of powers to the incumbent to marry by licence was interpreted by him as a commission to marry all comers, and of the 490 couples who were married by him in the following twenty-four years only 15 were resident as to one or both of the partners in the parish itself, (Chambers, 1957, p. 50). Of the rest, the marriage partners of 284 were drawn from different parishes, sometimes at considerable distances from one another. Samuel King of Cotes (Leics.) and Jane Trotter of Lincoln, Joseph Hinde of Bolsover and Mary Westley of Gamston (Notts.), Anthony Smith of Oulston (Yorks.) and Catherine Bland of Kelham (Notts.) had travelled far to meet one another, and having met decided to marry at the tiny village of Fledborough in Nottinghamshire. Perhaps there was a magic in the incumbent's name; the Reverend William Sweetapple. The local Gretna Green over which he presided so successfully for nearly a quarter of a century at least shows that there was no lack of matrimonial mobility for those who really wanted it.

There were other obstacles to marriage to which more weight should be given. Professor Ashton has pointed out that 'women in particular might remain single, not because of a shortage of men but because the candidates for matrimony were socially ineligible'. Preston—'Proud Preston'—subsisted, it was said, 'by many families of middling fortune ... and it is remarkable for old maids, because their families will not ally with tradesmen, and have not sufficient fortunes for gentlemen' (p. 5). And below the class in which social conditions weighed heavily were labourers and domestic servants living in, for whom marriage meant a great disturbance of their way of life and possible loss of their livelihood. According to the philosopher Hume, all masters discouraged 'the marrying of their male servants and admit not by any means the marriage of the female', an attitude deplored by Joseph Hanway, who asked why should these classes of people be prevented from marrying more than any other. It is interesting to note that Irish masters took an entirely different view. In the course of his Irish Tour Arthur Young roundly declared that marriage was 'certainly more general in Ireland than in England: I scarce ever found an unmarried farmer or cottar, but it is seen more in other classes, which with us do not marry at all; such as servants; the generality of foot-men and maids, in gentlemen's families, are married, a circumstance we very rarely see in England' (ii. 87). Literary evidence of this kind, however, must be taken with caution. Analysis of parish records points to a high level of nuptiality among the working population; celibacy among women in the villages of Bedfordshire was rare (not more than 5 per cent) as Dr Tranter has shown (1966, pp. 187–8), and the analysis of the age structure of the population of Lichfield clearly shows that the proportion of celibacy was low (Glass and Eversley, p. 182). Yet it must be conceded that the number of marriages in general was somewhat lower than it need have been, not so much for reasons of geographical mobility but rather because of social pressures in a graded society which was already very much under the influence of acquisitive values.

On the whole, however, the various restrictive influences that were brought to bear affected the age at, rather than the rate of, marriage. This was partly due to the imbalance in the age structure of the sexes. There was always an excess of male over female babies, probably in the ratio of 105 : 100, but since more boys died under the age of twenty than girls there was usually an excess of females by that age. However, mortality among wives was high and most women had a chance to marry, so that the propensity to marry was high in both sexes. Sir Gervase Clifton, the Nottinghamshire squire, had seven wives, and though no woman is on record as having as many husbands, there are two who have left their mark on the annals of nuptiality. The Wife of Bath confided to her companion as follows:

> 'Good Sirs, since I was twelve some years ago
> (Thanks to God that I am still alive)
> Of husbands at the church door, I've had five.'

And Bess of Hardwicke, a less fictional figure, had four husbands from the age of fourteen. Her marital career was unusual in another way; it began at the age of fourteen, which, according to Dr Hollingsworth's valuable study of the British aristocracy, was well below the average. He has collected data relating to nearly 2,000 legitimate children of kings, queens, dukes, and duchesses born between 1330 and 1939 and examined them by 'cohorts', that is, groups of individuals born in seven successive periods in the light of known dates regarding their marriage, offspring, and deaths. It seems that between the fourteenth and the end of the eighteenth century the mean age of dukes' daughters at first marriage rose from 17·1 to 24·7; in the same period the age of their sons at marriage had risen from 22·4 to 30·5. Correspondingly, the proportion who were spinsters at the age of 25 had risen from 15 to 46 per cent, and of bachelors from 50 to 80 per cent (Glass and Eversley, pp. 364-5).

A remarkably similar pattern was found by M. Henry, in his study of the ruling families of Geneva. The percentage single of those dying over 50 rose from 9 per cent for men and 2 per cent for women in the second half of the sixteenth century to 29 per cent for men and 29 per cent for women in the first half of the eighteenth century (Glass and Eversley, p. 114). We thus see that among these select social groups, the level of nuptiality was low and was getting lower as the acquisition of wealth became the accepted criterion of success.

If the low level of nuptiality seems to have been peculiar to the aristocracy the comparatively high age of marriage was common to all classes of the community. Evidence continues to multiply that in the seventeenth and eighteeth centuries the age at marriage of women in England was about 24, though it could rise, as Dr Wrigley has shown in his study of Colyton, as high as 30 after the plague of 1546 (1966, p. 81). The age of men was usually about two years higher. From a study of marriage allegations and certificates in Nottinghamshire and Gloucestershire between 1650 and 1750 it was found that farmers—yeomanry and husbandmen—married between 25 and 30; gentlemen about 26; and apprenticed workmen at almost the same age, except framework knitters among whom apprenticeship had largely lost its meaning, who married between 23 and 24 and chose slightly younger wives (Chambers, 1957, p. 52). Incidentally the lower age at marriage of the industrial workers may be especially significant, pointing to a tendency asserting itself with increasing strength as the advance of industrialization accelerated: the relative growth of the industrial population would impart some tendency for the mean age at marriage to fall, apart from any other influences that may have made for this result.

This, the relatively high age at marriage of women, is therefore the crux of the special characteristics of marriage in pre-idustrial England and indeed in Western Europe as a whole, while it is agreed that the age of marriage is one of the most important variables bearing upon reproduction rates. A mean age at first marriage for women of 22 (that of aristocratic brides in the early seventeenth century) could give rise to twice as many births in completed families as a mean age of marriage of 30 (as in the village of Colyton), owing to the high proportion of children born in the early years of marriage; and if the fall of six or seven years in the marriage age that Wrigley has found at Colyton between the last years of the seventeenth century and the early years of the nineteenth century (1966, p. 87) is found to be typical of the country as a whole, we have a significant pointer to one of the main causes of population growth in the eighteenth century.

SOCIAL AND ECONOMIC IMPLICATIONS

From what has been said, and it is only a brief outline of what could be said, it is clear that very significant changes had taken place in the marriage pattern of Western Europe in the thousand years that had elapsed since the fall of the Roman Empire. Marriage had become more stable, usually unbroken, except by the death of one of the partners, and was associated with a relatively low level of illegitimacy; celibacy for social reasons, both of men and women, was by no means uncommon; and most significantly of all, the age of marriage of girls appears to have almost doubled, that is from 12–15 in the late Roman Empire to 22–6 among the women of England and France in the eighteenth century.

The combination of high age at marriage, the existence of various social and institutional obstacles to high nuptiality, and at the same time a quite remarkable degree of geographical mobility laid the groundwork for a competitive and acquisitive society in which the ratio of resources to population was thereby kept in a favourable balance. It was the ideal instrument of self-aggrandizement for enterprising families and provided a hand-hold for those with means and opportunity to make their way to the top as well as a check to blind procreation of those at lower levels struggling for subsistence. While some rose, others fell, but the ineluctable circulation of the social elements went on. From the fifteenth century, the rise of substantial yeoman families, often at the expense of poorer families, laying field to field and farm to farm and pushing their way into the ranks of the gentry, provided a scaffolding of immense strength and energy to the English rural economy. Along with the more enterprising landlords they enclosed whole villages for sheep in the wool boom of the fifteenth century, and changed over to the production of meat and corn under the influence of the rising prices in the sixteenth and seventeenth centuries. They built a scatter of substantial houses and palatial halls over the length and breadth of England, providing thereby a market for the products of an industrial expansion which was once accorded the name of an Industrial Revolution. At the same time, the endless circulation of footloose labour brought a tide of hungry and active boys and girls to the towns, and above all to London, which, by the end of the seventeenth century, was providing the means for food and shelter for one-tenth of the entire nation. There was, it would seem, from the fifteenth century a surging onward and upward of the human hive and every social class was involved in it. Among the upper ranks of the social pyramid the struggle was all the keener as a result of the comparatively high fertility rate of the upper classes. Hollingsworth has suggested that in the second half of the sixteenth century the families of the peerage were reproducing themselves at a hitherto unparalleled rate (Glass and Eversley, pp. 370–1); and since the rule of primogeniture required that younger sons should make their own way in the world, the pressure for entrance into the professional classes was increased from the top just as the yeomanry were challenging them for a place in the ranks of the gentry from below. Professor Stone, in his study of the period (pp. 24–9), tells us that between 1500 and 1700 the armigerous gentry probably rose from 5,000 to 15,000, and the classes above them rose by almost the same proportion while the population merely doubled. At the same time, the number of attorneys in the Court of Common Pleas more than quadrupled between 1578 and 1633 and by 1688 Gregory King reckoned the entire legal profession at 10,000. There must

c

also have been 3,000 or 4,000 local and central office-holders in 1690, says Stone, with incomes over £100 per year—a veritable army of Excise Men, Hearth-Tax Collectors, Customs Officers, Treasury Officials, etc. Altogether if we include merchants, clergy, and officers in the army and navy, there existed a total of 65,000 families of gentry and officials with an aggregate annual income of more than £4½ million by the end of the seventeenth century. The new middle class provided a superstructure of skill and enterprise incomparably stronger than that of the underdeveloped countries of today and fully capable of grasping the opportunities that economic expansion offered.

Of course it is not possible to say how far the marriage pattern contributed to this, but the examination of particular cases certainly suggests that we should not ignore it. Thus the spiral of social mobility was mounted, sometimes by hard work, often by lucky marriages; and the pattern set by the landed classes gave the clue to the middle classes and the new industrialists. The part played by marriage in floating industrial enterprise would repay more attention than it has received. We can think of John Wilkinson and Matthew Boulton, both of whom made lucrative marriages twice in their lives, and we may be reminded of the latter's advice to young men about to embark on a commercial career: 'Don't marry for money but marry where money is.' This advice fell on willing ears. An examination of the provincial press would yield a heavy crop of examples of founders of local firms who advertised their origin by proudly announcing their engagement or marriage to 'an elegant young lady of genteel fortune', to 'a most accomplished young lady with a fortune of £7,000', or 'the amiable widow of Mr Spicer of London possessed of a large fortune' (*Nottingham Journal*, 2 July 1768; 24 July 1773; 31 March 1770). We would dearly like to know how far down the social scale this devotion to the prudential marriage is to be found. The overwhelming popularity of Richardson's novel *Pamela* shows that many thousands of readers were vicarious participants in her brilliant success in bringing to the altar the young man who had so ardently pursued her. She saved the precious jewel of her virtue, she says, until she could get the price that she had set on it: a lawful marriage before two witnesses in the parish church near Stamford. Apparently, in the village of Slough the novel was read in instalments as they appeared by the blacksmith to the villagers gathered

round his forge, and when he came to the triumphant issue of
Pamela's adventures by lawful marriage, they were so overjoyed
that they rushed out and celebrated the event with a merry peal
on the church bells.

We should not therefore be surprised that marriage played such
an important part in the literature of the times. The plays of the
Restoration, and the novels of the eighteenth century from Defoe
to Jane Austen, are embroideries, more or less sedate and studied,
on the theme of marriage. Amongst the gentry the act of courtship
was a highly sophisticated branch of social relations. From the
time the young lady left her finishing school at seventeen or
eighteen, she was in the market for a husband, and it was her
father's business to find the best that his estate could afford. Negoti-
ations went forward with the formality of an alliance between
sovereign states, and correspondence was exchanged on the question of jointures and portions between the father and eligible
young men, sometimes for years before a final decision was taken.
Even in the case of a small squire like Nicholas Blundell of Crosby
in Lancashire, who could only dispose of an income of a few
hundred a year, the marriage of his eldest daughter Molly occupied
a period of six years, during which time two suitors favoured
by the father were firmly rejected by the young lady, albeit with
tears of distress at having to disappoint her father's wishes, and
numerous others were considered and rejected for one reason or
another. All this took place, of course, through the medium of a
series of balls, soirées, and family celebrations, when the young
people went through the stately motions of the quadrille and
the gavotte, forms of the terpsichorean art that were specifically
adapted to the requirements of courtship in an age when it was
pursued not for passion but for property. The young people could
take stock of one another in the course of this pattern of courtly
advance and withdrawal, of genuflexions and pirouettings, while
the elders could do their matrimonial arithmetic in the window-
seats. And this would, of course, be both complex and prolonged.
Nicholas Blundell had only a small income but he had two
daughters, and he had to spend nearly £150 on dresses for them
on their 'coming out'. They still looked 'graceless country lasses',
we are told, in spite of their finery; 'but the squire knew that
what they carried on their backs was more important in the
marriage market than what peeped out from under their bonnets',

and it is happy to be able to record that after this amiable charade had gone on for five or six years both daughters found husbands to their liking, and the squire was blessed with a little Blundell by blood though not by name to carry the family on (Blundell, Chapters XII–XIV).

If this was the pattern for the squirearchy and the ranks above them, how far did it go down in the social scale? The artisans, the skilled workmen, the yeomen, and the husbandmen had a similar period of waiting before they could enter the married state. How was it occupied? No one can tell us. We get gobbets of facts and figures, items of a measurable magnitude as Professor Clapham described them; but the pangs of flesh and blood which the young people must have experienced escape us. Jacob, we are told, waited seven years for Rachael; but our country swains waited hardly less for their Annes and Abigails and Marthas. We have to go to the novelists, especially Defoe and Richardson, for a hint of this unknown country of the heart.

But for a glimpse into the depths where the labourer and his lass settled their affairs we must go to the ploughboy poet, Robert Burns. 'Ay fond kiss and then we sever', sang the poet, usually leaving behind a more substantial token of his successful pursuit. In fact, out of his thirteen children, eight are known to have been illegitimate. Perhaps Bobby Burns was more irresistible than other men, especially Englishmen, where the bastardly rate was comparatively low, anyway this was Scotland, where whisky and bad weather may have breached barriers more readily than in England, which has a record for moderation in all things.

But the marriage institution I have been describing is a European, not a specifically English, phenomenon. If, as I have suggested, it exercised a favourable influence on the process of capital accumulation and the development of entrepreneurial attitudes, how do we account for the difference in the rate of progress in capitalist development in England compared with the rest of Western Europe?

The answer seems to lie in two fields of development which distinguished English practice and English social behaviour from most of her neighbours: first, the greater productivity of English agriculture which raised the effective demand of the English farming community for non-agricultural goods, particularly houses, clothes, fuel, implements, etc.; secondly, to the greater emphasis on commercial and industrial objectives which characterized English social ambitions compared with the more feudal outlook that prevailed, for instance, among the French bourgeoisie.

On the subject of agricultural progress, I think there are few who would deny that the operations of Malthusian direct checks to population growth were less pronounced in England than in France, at least from 1650; and that whatever may have been the cause of the slow growth of English population it was no longer due to the direct impact of famine, as it was in France for a century after that date. Briefly, we can say that the advance in the well-being of the English farming population had been so substantial that the direct effect of harvest failure in the form of death from starvation is extremely difficult to detect at least from 1650 if not before. In contrast, we may cite the evidence presented by M. Goubert of the continued menace of famine which hovered over the French peasant community in his study of the Beauvaisis. In no case, he says (1956, pp. 67–8), could a holding of less than twelve hectares assure its occupants of the slightest trace of economic independence. Three-quarters of the peasantry remained well below this level, hence the majority suffered from almost continuous undernourishment. During lean years they had to resign themselves to dying in their thousands for lack of food. I do not think it is possible to find any parallel to this in English demographic history after 1650. On the contrary, the complaint that was most frequently made in England was how to dispose of the grain surplus. The pangs of plenty suffered by the English farmer were heard more consistently and received more attention than the pangs of hunger on the part of the poor.

The progress of agriculture, however, should not be allowed to take the entire credit for the greater prosperity of the English labouring population, for there is also the fact of the differential burden of taxation that was borne by the French compared with the English. M. Goubert estimates that the peasants of Beauvaisis had to pay something like a half of their product in central, local, or feudal taxation (1956, p. 67). The contrast with the more fortunate lot of the Englishman cannot be better expressed than by the sixteenth-century pamphleteer recently resuscitated by Professor Fisher (1961, p. 13), who exhorted his fellow countrymen to count their blessings as Englishmen. Speaking of the continental peasantry he says;

They paye till theire bones rattle in their skin: and thou [Englishman] layest up for thy sonne and heir. Thou are twise or thrise in thy lifetime called uppon to healpe thy countrye with a subsidie or contribution: and they daily pay and never cease. Thou livest like a Lorde and they like dogges. . . . Oh, if thou knewest thou Englishe man in what welth thou livest and in how plentifull a countrye: thou wouldest vii times of the day fall flat on thy face before God, and geve him thanks that thou wart born an Englishman and not a french pezant, nor an Italyan, nor Almane.

If the feudal structure of society had the effect of bleeding the French agricultural community of resources that, in the more commercial setting of England, would have been available for consumption and investment, the same influence operated to deflect the ends of prudential marriage on the part of the French bourgeoisie into channels that were relatively subordinate in the list of priorities open to their English counterparts. In France, marriage was at least as prudential as in England, but the object was not directed to the same extent towards commercial or industrial ends, rather towards acquisition of an office, pension, or some other form of fixed investment. In France, as in England, snobbery was at its priest-like task of strengthening the sinews of the Acquisitive Society. But acquisitiveness in France took its own characteristic form reflecting the feudal structure within which it operated. In both countries there were complaints of the shortage of suitable husbands for the daughters of the landed gentry; in France this was said to be due to the deliberate choice of celibacy on the part of younger sons. In England, younger sons had a wider range of choice; they could become professional men and marry into professional as well as mercantile families (Habakkuk, 1950, p. 24). The usual alternative a French nobleman might consider was to buy an office for which competition from the middle classes was keen and ruthless.

As Louis XIV was informed by his Minister, one of the greatest prerogatives of the King of France was that 'as soon as the King creates an office, God creates at the same moment a fool to buy it' (Blacker, pp. 54–5); and French bourgeois parents seem to have gone to greater lengths than those of England to make the appropriate sacrifice required by their social ambitions. This involved corresponding sacrifices on the part of married couples, if this extract from a French play of 1706 bears any relationship to the historical realities, (Blacker, p. 56):

> 'I say, in a word, if you listen to me,
> All excesses are fatal to us bourgeoisie.
> We must on occasion from pleasure abstain,
> Having only those children we well can maintain.
> 'Tis better to nurture with care but one child,
> Than produce half a dozen and let 'em run wild,
> Till finding themselves of their parents bereft,
> They discover for each there is deuced little left.'

Even among the larger bourgeoisie both in commerce and industry, we are told that the motives for avoiding the necessity of dividing the family fortune were the same, namely to concentrate the family resources on the purchase of a lucrative office. The same motive operated in the competition for professional advancement, which was barred to all but the wealthy. Social background was relatively a secondary consideration. In the case of the doctors, for instance, money alone counted, the only exceptions being made to exclude unbaptized Jews, bastards, and the sons of hangmen. The reason why the last were deemed unsuitable for the profession of doctor was due not to social considerations, but professional jealousy, since hangmen were supposed to have esoteric knowledge of human anatomy, and were sometimes consulted in preference to regular surgeons and physicians. The bourgeois who wished his son to rise in the medical profession had every incentive to conserve his capital by limiting his family. As one bourgeois wife said to another, 'Jesu, how I dread having so many children' (Blacker, pp. 57-9).

In France, therefore, the prudential aspect of marriage was practised, at least among the bourgeoisie, as assiduously as in England, maybe more so; but the consequences were less favourable to the processes of economic growth. The effective demand of the English agricultural community was greater as a result of lighter taxation and higher agricultural productivity, and the objectives of bourgeois prudence were less narrowly circumscribed by bureaucratic office-seeking; although in its essential characteristic the institution of marriage in both countries was consciously directed towards accumulation for social and economic ends which could not fail to strengthen the sinews of nascent industrial society.

I think we can now return to the question posed by Professor Hajnal that sparked off this discussion: 'Could the uniquely European marriage pattern', he asks, 'help to explain how the groundwork was laid for the uniquely European take-off to modern growth?' In the light of the evidence submitted I think we must concede it provides at least a part of the explanation. Its contribution lies not exclusively in providing a differential level of fertility leading to a slower growth of population and higher resources *per capita*, although that was certainly important; it led also to the building up of a social system that was based on the autonomy of the individual family unit, free from dependence on kin, and accustomed to accept the sole responsibility for the bearing and nurture of children. This belonged to the parents alone. In this way was laid the groundwork of a society which learned not only the economic but also the demographic techniques that made continuous economic growth possible. To this extent Hajnal's thesis appears to be valid and important.

I think, however, it is necessary to add that by the middle of the eighteenth century the role of marriage in the gathering tempo of economic advance was changing. The factors of restraint which constituted its essential character were being weakened with important results on fertility and the birth-rate. Two circumstances combined to effect this important change; first, the disproportionate growth of the industrial sector of the population would impart a general trend towards a lower age of marriage as a statistical characteristic of the community as a whole. If we are to find evidence of the falling age of marriage we must look in the first place to the towns and the industrial villages; but by the early nineteenth century, if not before, it seems to have also reached the rural population, now more generally living in cottages rather than in the houses of their masters. The second was the erosion of ecclesiastical influences on the relations of the sexes, reflected in a rise in the proportion of bastardy and pre-marital conception. In the course of the century, the incidence of the latter probably doubled, but the evidence suggests that recorded bastardy may have risen four or five times in the same period (see Chapter 3). These two factors mark the end of an epoch in the history of European marriage which began in the last centuries of the Roman Empire and inaugurated a new phase in its evolution, the unfolding of which continues to influence our society down to the present day.

3
Marriage and Fertility

IN the preceding chapters, two main propositions regarding population change have been advanced: first, that instead of responding mechanically to economic change, as is often assumed, it appears to have followed a fluctuating trend not obviously or directly related, in a causal sense, to economic factors as reflected in price; in other words, changes in the long-term trend of population appear to have sprung from forces that were, from an economic point of view, fortuitous. Secondly, that the institution of marriage, as it existed in the Christian West, was peculiarly favourable to economic growth and development, especially through the comparatively late age at which, on the whole, it tended to take place. This is not to say, of course, that the age at marriage was immutable over the centuries in a country such as England, nor that fertility levels within marriage, in society at large, or between different socio-economic groups, were unvaryingly uniform.

These important considerations form the subject matter of this chapter, but it is best to begin with a brief review of the parish registers as a source for the study of marriage and fertility, and of the methods that have been applied to them. To begin with, prior to 1753 it is impossible to make a valid statement about the rate of marriage from the study of a single parish, although this is sometimes attempted. For example, in two villages investigated by Mr Laslett and Mr Harrison, the rates are given in one case as 10–13.3 marriages per thousand and in the other as 6.9 (pp. 173, 176). No explanation is offered and one presumes none can be given. But the various factors that might account for discrepancies of this kind can be listed. Certain religious groups such as Catholics, Jews, and Quakers could obtain licences to solemnize marriages in their own places of worship; some extreme Presbyterians did not indeed believe in formal marriage at all; parsons were not always as honest or conscientious as they should have been and more especially, some were more popular than others. Until the passing of Lord Hardwicke's Marriage Act of 1753 there was nothing to prevent the intending couple going to the parson or church of their choice, wherever this might be. Hence the marriages registered in a single parish need not by any means reflect the number of marriages entered into by the parishioners who were resident there. To try to calculate the rate of marriage for a single parish is therefore a labour in vain; but if the marriages by banns and by special licence for an area, say, of a radius of 10 miles, can be related to the size of the total population, it is possible to calculate a rate which may be regarded with respect. Even then it would be necessary to make some adjustment for the nonconformist marriages in the area; and the size of the adjustment could be established only by close investigation on the spot.

The difficulties in the way of calculating the rate of births to which the marriages gave rise is even greater. The Church authorities could bring some degree of pressure through the Court of the Ordinary upon parents to bring their offspring to the font. A charge in the Archdeacon's Court might be preferred against them if they delayed more than a fortnight; but it was backed by no penalty, only a reprimand. At the worst, and very rarely, it might amount to excommunication, i.e. the refusal of the cup at Communion for the persistently recalcitrant. In the elongated parishes of Lincolnshire, for instance, where marshland farmers might be 5 miles away from the church on the edge of the higher land, the bringing of the babies to the font was a less pressing problem than the disposal of a corpse in the graveyard; and to overcome this difficulty, the family might be baptized *en masse* at a suitable time.

There were other possible loopholes through which unrecorded births could slip. It is unlikely that all bastard children were entered as such in the registers, though most investigators think that the record is realistic at least until the last decades of the eighteenth century. Still-births would usually not be recorded at all; infants who lived a few hours might be entered as 'chrisom child' though the numbers are suspiciously few; and what can be said of abortions and infanticide, of which there is no record at all? The number of entries, therefore, in the baptism register represents only a proportion of the actual births and a still smaller proportion of the conceptions.

For these reasons, students of the parish registers have devised a number of ratios for converting baptisms to births, as well, of course, as burials to deaths. The difficulties of this operation are very grave since the coverage of parish registration varied a great deal from county to county and also from one period to another. I cannot see that any useful purpose would be served by entering into the technicalities of this problem, but it may be noticed in passing that the latest national calculations made by Deane and Cole are based for better or for worse upon the average conversion ratios derived from the calculations of Dr Brownlee (pp. 107–9). These have been severely criticized, but any alternative ratio would be open to the same criticism, and in any case, the problem was not as serious in the eighteenth century as it became in the early nineteenth, when the strain placed upon the ecclesiastical organization, owing to drastic changes in the distribution as well as in the actual size of population, led to something like a breakdown of registration. In fact, if a sufficiently large number of entries are examined, especially if they are drawn from contiguous areas, and include examples of a variety of communities, urban as well as rural, agricultural as well as industrial, significant results can be obtained. By aggregating the entries in the registers it is possible to observe the general trend of the three variables of baptisms, burials, and marriages; and by comparing them with one another and with independent estimates of the population at different times it is possible to obtain rates of change that are at least indications of probabilities, if no more.

This method of inquiry obviously labours under inherent limitations; because it yields only approximate indications of crude vital rates, it can tell us nothing about age structure, size of families, length of child-bearing period, and of intervals between births. For these and other more detailed aspects we have to resort to other methods, in particular to the method of family reconstitution developed in the first place in France by M. Henry and now practised by students of demography in many parts of this country and in particular by a number of investigators working under the direction of Dr Wrigley at Cambridge. The method consists basically in tracing family relationships from the baptisms to marriages and burials, where these can be found. Owing to the limited number of christian names, problems of identification often arise; and on account of the constant movement of population into and out of the village, the chances of omission of names from the Anglican registers and the paucity of nonconformist registers, there is no possibility of getting more than representative samples from any single set of registers. But when this is done with all the rigorous attention to accurate recording which demographers have evolved, there can be no doubt that this method opens up a new and exciting phase in English historical demography. The same kind of methodology can sometimes be applied to specific and therefore limited social groups on which precise and detailed demographic information happens to be available, as Mr Hollingsworth has shown in his remarkable work on the demography of the British aristocracy.

What can we learn from the various methods of parish-register analysis about patterns of fertility in pre-industrial England and the factors that accounted for them?

Let us begin with some examples based on the aggregative method of analysis, that is, by simply summing baptisms, marriages, and burials and comparing their incidence over time. Dr Eversley has analysed the remarkable response of a number of Worcestershire villages to the onslaught of mortality in the notorious epidemic years of 1725–9. It was a period of wet summers, hard winters, food shortages, and fevers, and in twelve parishes roughly within a radius of 5 miles of Bromsgrove, there was a huge excess of burials over baptisms; at the height of the epidemic baptisms declined owing to mortality among actual and potential mothers; but as soon as the epidemic was over there was an upsurge of marriages and a rise of the crude birth-rate to 42 per thousand or more. Eversley calculates that the turn-over of jobs and tenancies would have risen from 4 to 8·8 per cent per annum, providing opportunities for advancement and for living accommodation which would be reflected in this stampede to the altar. An observed increase of the marriage rate from 10·35 to 14·34 per 1,000 in 1730–4 would, he thinks, represent two extra marriages, or re-marriages, and two 'anticipated' marriages; and by 1735–44 the rate had fallen to 8·46 (Glass and Eversley, pp. 408–9). This example represents the kind of response the population made in a rapidly expanding area in the neighbourhood of Birmingham in a period of prosperity. The recovery was astonishing; nevertheless, he says, it took more than 25 years for the population to recover the position of 1725. But it would be a younger population than would otherwise have been the case. This fact, together with the improved conditions making for greater expectation of life, must be taken into account in explaining the expansion of the 1740s and '50s.

The period of 25 years mentioned by Eversley required to recover the position of 1725 calls for further comment. It coincides remarkably with the findings of Dr Tranter for thirty villages of Bedfordshire, though in this case the long-term effect was attributable not only to the set-back of 1727–30 but also to bad epidemic years in 1740–2 and 1747–8. Had it not been for these, the earlier losses, he thinks, would have been made up in 10 years; but as a result of the combined effect of these various set-backs, the population total did not reach its pre-epidemic level until 1752, a period of 26 years (1966, pp. 81, 88). In the case of a number of Nottinghamshire villages the loss was made up in about 10 years, but the town of Nottingham did not make up its arrears by its own natural increase, for over 30 years (Chambers, 1957, p. 35; 1960, p. 122). If, then, we may postulate a period of 25 years during which urban-population growth and in some cases rural-population growth was catching up on the losses of the epidemic years, we are faced with a situation in which in the second quarter of the century the remarkable resilience of fertility was scarcely able to hold its own against repeated crises of mortality. At least, this appears to hold true for the regions mentioned; it is not known whether the same could be said of other areas (e.g. Lancashire or Yorkshire), where conditions may have been more favourable.

We may now turn to the second important result of the aggregative study of the registers. This relates to the differential fertility rate of industrial and agricultural parishes as illustrated by the Nottinghamshire study, which shows the consistently higher fertility of the partially industrialized villages, compared with those that were wholly agricultural. By dividing marriages into baptisms, their comparative fertility following the disastrous years 1727–9 is shown in Table 3 (Chambers, 1957, p. 53) overleaf:

TABLE 3

Differential Fertility in Eighteenth-century Nottinghamshire

	1730-9	1740-9	1750-9	1760-9
Agricultural villages	3·3	3·3	3·4	3·7
Industrial villages	3·9	4·4	4·8	4·5

	1770-9	1780-9	1790-9
Agricultural villages	3·6	3·7	3·7
Industrial villages	4·8	4·7	4·8

On the basis of these figures, the fertility of industrial parishes appears to have been between 20 and 30 per cent higher than that of agricultural parishes. As was shown in the last chapter, there is some evidence that the industrial population married a little earlier—two years in the case of the men—one year in the case of the women—but in addition to this explanation, we should also consider the factors within marriage that could contribute to this result: for example, shorter intervals between births and greater expectation of life of the mother when living conditions, in terms of wages and prices, and cottage accommodation were good, although the necessary research for this (which would require family reconstitution) has not yet been done. It is also possible that migration played its part in accounting for these results: newly married couples may have moved into the industrial villages before their families had arrived, with the result that bonus baptisms were added to the registers of the industrial villages without a corresponding addition to the marriage registers. To that extent the differential fertility of the industrial villages may be illusory, and we must keep this in mind when we meet the same situation in the Lancashire and West Riding parishes which were similarly drawing recruits from neighbouring rural areas. But even with this important qualification I think one must allow that the evidence points to a higher level of fertility among the industrial population at the time and to a confirmation of the view that the industrial population grew not only as a result of transference of population by migration but also by a higher rate of self-recruitment.

Thirdly, existing parish studies based on aggregative methods of analysis have been re-examined from a somewhat original point of view by Professor Pentland of Manitoba University in a paper to which I should like to refer briefly here, and more extensively in Chapter 5. His first important comment (p. 7) is that the several series of absolute totals of baptisms exhibit a marked volatility, i.e. short-term movements upward and downward, which tends to be obscured when attention is confined to the national figures collected at the time of the first census by John Rickman and used as the basis of calculations by Talbot Griffith and others in their studies of population in the eighteenth century (see Chapter 5). Furthermore, following through the behaviour of the series over time reveals a still more significant characteristic; he observes a 'lack of relationship at any reasonable interval between baptisms and the apparent availability of parents [which is] so pronounced that a social rather than a biological explanation for the fluctuation of baptisms is needed' (p. 12). These findings imply the existence of a population able to recognize economic opportunities when it saw them, and ready to adjust marriage and child-bearing propensities more quickly, and to a greater extent, than is commonly allowed by those who assume that in the pre-industrial world birth-rates were more or less constant at the limit of biological potential.

Professor Pentland is raising the question of controlled fertility in response to economic conditions, and there is no doubt some measure of truth in this view. However a qualification needs to be made at this point; the society in which this responsiveness is supposed to have operated was still essentially agrarian in character. Three-fifths of the labouring population still derived a livelihood from the soil, and a very large proportion of these would be servants living in. Another large proportion of the labour force was domestic servants as well as apprenticed workmen forbidden to marry within the period of their indentures. This being the case, pre-industrial nuptiality, and as a consequence fertility, was probably at least as much determined by social institutions and habits as by conscious calculations of economic advantage, at least until the obvious advance of industrialization and rapid growth of cottage labour at the expense of indoor agricultural labour in the later eighteenth century reduced traditional barriers to marriage and opened the door to a more rapid expansion of the labour force. In some areas of course, these conditions obtained at an earlier date, notably in districts of equal partition of holdings, which permitted the proliferation of families on smallholdings; and in the industrialized villages of the Midlands and the north-west, particularly Lancashire and the West Riding. For such areas, as will be shown later, there is indeed some evidence to suggest that the barriers to expansion had already been lowered long before the period traditionally alloted to the demographic revolution of the last quarter of the eighteenth century.

On the basis of the aggregative studies so far discussed, three important suggestions seem to emerge:

1. As a result of high mortality in the epidemic years, especially 1725–9, urban and in some cases rural populations spent up to twenty-five years recovering the position of 1725. In the areas discussed, fertility was hardly able to hold its own against repeated crises of mortality, although it is not known, at present, whether the same sort of check to population growth was also operative elsewhere in the same period.

2. There existed a differential fertility pattern between industrial and agricultural populations (on the basis of the Nottinghamshire figures), and the industrial population tended to have a higher rate of self-recruitment.

3. Economic and social conditions affected nuptiality and fertility, although there is likely to have been an element of inertia arising out of social structure, institutions, and habits. These factors are, however, likely to have been eroded over time, as industrialism offered wider and on the whole more secure opportunities of earning a living.

Before we arrive at firm conclusions however, especially in the matter of the responsiveness of the population as a whole to complex and changing circumstances, we need to look more closely at the behaviour of the fertility variable as far as present research permits. At some points, we can take the inquiry rather further than the above-mentioned aggregative studies permit. Recent studies of marriage and, in particular, fertility patterns have enriched our knowledge considerably, although it cannot yet be said that anything like a clear picture has emerged. In particular, I should like to take this opportunity to review recent evidence on class or status differences in fertility, on the conscious control of births within marriage together with the apparent importance of psychological factors in this process, and on changes in the incidence of illegitimacy and pre-marital conceptions.

STATUS DIFFERENCES IN FERTILITY AND FAMILY SIZE

If we take the child-bearing period as the 24 years lying between 15 and 49 and the average number of years of married life as 15 or 16, we should expect about 7 or 8 births per family at least. But the evidence points to lower average fertility; including childless and broken as well as fertile and complete marriages, perhaps no more than 4 or 5 children on the average, at least until the last quarter of the eighteenth century.

Moreover, family size varied between different socio-economic groups. For instance, an Elizabethan survey of 450 poor families of Norwich shows that households consisted usually of parents and 2 or 3 children, at the time of the count; whereas the well-to-do merchants of Norwich and Exeter had 4.25 and 4.7 children respectively (Pound, p. 142). No doubt differential infant mortality played its part in accounting for this discrepancy, as did the fact that poor men and their wives could not expect to live long enough to have as many children as their richer neighbours. Indeed, contemporary surveys often reveal a large number of second marriages. In Clayworth 35.5 per cent of all children had lost one parent, whilst in Manchester in the 1650s a quarter of the marriages were between widows and widowers and half of the brides and bridegrooms marrying for the first time were reported as fatherless (Laslett, pp. 95, 260–1).

How far the Norwich finding may also be taken to reflect a genuine fertility difference is of course, problematic; but the evidence for the peerage is distinctly less ambiguous. Both in regard to age at marriage and conditions of life, aristocrats had an advantage over the lower social classes that was reflected in a considerable disparity in fertility. Between 1550 and 1625 the sons and grandsons of peers married at 25 or 26, the daughters at 20 or 21, probably two or even three years younger than those of husbandmen and labourers. This might be expected to make a difference of one or possibly two births per marriage, since fertility was particularly high in the first years of marriage. Moreover it is reasonable to suppose that there would be relatively fewer marriages broken by death and therefore a higher average period for child-bearing among the peerage. Whatever the reason, the fertility of the peerage after the period 1680–1729 was remarkably high until well into the nineteenth century, as Table 4 shows (Glass and Eversley, 1965, p. 372):

TABLE 4
Ducal Families: Female Fertility, 20–49, Births per Married Woman

Cohort Born

1680–1729	4·98
1730–79	7·29
1780–1829	7·91
1830–79	5·67
1880–1939	4·81

With the aid of Dr Tranter's researches into the villages of Bedfordshire, we can go a little further in this inquiry. There, the average number of baptisms per marriage hovered about $3\frac{1}{2}$–4, and the figure for completed marriages exhibited a slight rise from 5·1 to 5·16 baptisms between 1690–1720 and 1750–75, although one parish, Cardington, attained 6·17. The mean age at first marriage for completed unions of the second period was for men 27, for women 24, and the proportion of childless marriages was 10 per cent (1966, p. 150–4). Even including the exceptional case of Cardington these fertility levels are considerably lower than those of the aristocracy, and it will be noticed that there is no evidence here of a similar sudden jump in fertility in the post-1750 period.

Additionally, there is some reason to think that differential fertility may be found *within* the village population itself. In a personal communication, Tranter indicates that 13 marriages of farmers in Cardington for 1782 produced 92 children, giving an average of 7·08 baptisms per marriage. He has shown earlier that 51 completed cottagers' marriages in Cardington produced an average of only 5·41, and this was higher than in any other Bedfordshire village examined. This meant that the average size of cottage households at the time of the local listing of 1782 was only 4·18, and the mean number of children residing at home was 2·27. One-third of their children, he suggests, would normally die before reaching the age of twenty-one, and one child would have left home (1967, pp. 267–8, 275–7).

Are we to infer from the smaller size of the completed family of the cottage labourer that either a large number of pregnancies ended negatively or that birth control was practised? Tranter himself is not inclined to accept the latter alternative. The reason for the difference, he thinks, was that the farmers' wives had a somewhat longer child-bearing period (i.e. the interval between the last and first birth which he finds was 10·77 years) and, more significantly, shorter intervals between births, possibly due to the longer period of lactation that was customary among labourers' wives (1966, pp. 275–6). We are back again, therefore, with the fact of poverty and hard conditions of life making for lower fertility. Even so, the possibility of deliberate regulation of fertility according to circumstances deserves further consideration in the light of recent work.

EVIDENCE OF FAMILY LIMITATION

G. C. Coulton (p. 244) long ago reminded us of the indictment brought against the peasantry by the Franciscan Alvarus Pelagius in the early fourteenth century; that 'they often abstain from knowing their own wives lest children should be born, fearing that they could not bring up so many, under pretext of poverty'. For eighteenth-century France M. Goubert has discovered that the mean interval between births was only twenty months in a Breton parish as against thirty observed in South-West France, 'a difference that cannot be due to chance' and which he attributes to the greater powers of the confessional in Britanny (1968, pp. 597–8). It is therefore not improbable that family limitation could occur in Protestant England when special circumstances seemed to demand it. Some evidence has been unearthed recently by Dr Wrigley (1966) for the Devonshire village of Colyton.

As one might expect, Wrigley finds that an important regulator of fertility was the age at marriage, which appears to have fluctuated over time. From 1560 to 1646 the mean age of women at first marriage was between 26 and 27; in the period 1647–59 it rose to 30 and remained so, with little change, until 1719. During this period the female marriage age was actually two years higher than that of the men. From 1720 the female age at marriage tended to go down, and by 1825 it had fallen to 23·3. Whereas in 1647–1719 only 4 per cent of the brides were in their teens and 40 per cent were over 30, by the first quarter of the nineteenth century 25 per cent of the brides were in their teens and only 7 per cent were over 30 (pp. 87–8). There had obviously been a marked shift towards earlier marriage. Such a change in the mean age of marriage, Wrigley thinks, provided scope for a very wide range of rates of increase or decrease of population. 'In marriages not prematurely interrupted by death, an average age at first marriage for women of, say, 24 might well produce two more children than marriages contracted at an average of, say, 29.' Between the two extremes of 23·3 in 1825–37 and 30·7 in 1700–1 a difference in the size of family by 2 could easily follow (p. 88).

The importance of these statements scarcely needs emphasizing, but even more significant in this context is the evidence suggesting the regulation of fertility within marriage. In Wrigley's words, 'any changes on the fertility side of population history of Colyton which arose from changes in the mean age of first marriage were considerably amplified by changes within marriage'. Between 1560 and 1629 age-specific marital fertility rates were high, pointing to a mean completed family size of 7·3 for brides married by the age of 24, and 5·7 for those married by 29. There was a marked decline from about 1630, a decline that became more pronounced after the renewal of the plague in 1646. 'The change from a high to a low level of fertility within these families was abrupt and complete'; a fall, in fact, to 5·0 and 3·3 respectively for the two age groups mentioned (pp. 88–9, 92, 97). Notably, there occurred a marked rise in the interval between the penultimate and the last birth which 'is typical of a community beginning to practise family limitation' (p. 94).

It has sometimes been supposed that the intuitive reaction of the population after a heavy loss of life is to increase fertility and to fill the gaps created by death (p. 92), but this does not appear to have been the case at Colyton. The numbers are, of course, small, but the picture is none the less suggestive. Fertility rates apparently dropped sharply and immediately to the levels which were to be characteristic of Colyton for the next two generations, although the women in question had displayed a fertility well above the average in the period before the swingeing losses of 1646. In fact only 18 per cent of women marrying under 30 between 1647 and 1719 and living right through the fertile period had families of 6 children or more, compared with 55 per cent in the period 1560–1625, 48 per cent in 1720–69, and 60 per cent between 1770 and 1837 (p. 97).

As a warning against a too easy acceptance of deliberate family limitation we should not omit to mention the footnote in which Wrigley draws attention to Creighton's invocation of the tradition that plague was associated with sterility in the surviving female population (p. 92). Nevertheless, after a consideration of all other possibilities he leaves little room for doubt that not only was there restriction of births within marriage, but that, in view of the rise in age of women at first marriage, a catastrophe such as a sharp attack of plague may have had an adverse effect upon the *propensity* to marry and have children. This important suggestion is worth pursuing further.

It is possible that the same factor may help to account for the failure of population to recover from the setbacks of the plagues of the fourteenth century. The Black Death of 1349 is generally believed to have been followed by further virulent outbreaks in 1361, 1369, and 1375, but it has recently been argued by Dr Bean that these subsequent sporadic attacks were too localized and scattered to account for the strange phenomenon of a hundred years of population stagnation, when economic conditions might have been expected to have the opposite effect. Land was now plentiful and prices were low. In terms of the ratio between population and subsistence, the peasantry were enjoying a golden age; but the population refused to rise. In a recent contribution of great interest Professor Thrupp has hinted at a psychological factor that should not be overlooked; after referring to the spread of disease as a result of the movement of the peasantry and traders from village to village and market town to market town, she says (p. 118) 'to the extent that migrations were aimless, or motivated by moods of fear, despair, desire to enter the Church or *otherwise to evade family responsibilities*' (my italics), we have a cultural interpretation of the phenomenon of demographic stagnation.

Professor Chevalier, the distinguished French demographer, would go further. Speaking of the puzzling phenomenon of demographic stagnation in France in the nineteenth century he writes: 'During the years following the wars of the Revolution and Empire the birth-rate declined, and some years, fell below the death-rate.' Demographers and economists who first became aware of it about 1856 found it hard to believe, and when asked to explain it had to confess their ignorance. 'And we have to repeat this confession of ignorance,' he says. De Tocqueville attributed it to the political instability following the French Revolution, which he saw as 'the cause of the lasting social and demographic disturbances in France'. He goes on, 'and the social and demographic repercussions of revolutions like those of 1830 and 1848 have been incomparably greater than their political consequences; their extent cannot fail to surprise one'. Between 1815 and 1848 fertility diminished, increased again to about 1861 (a period of political stability), and only began to fall again in 1865. 'This is, indeed, one of the more curious problems of the demographic evolution of nineteenth century France' (Glass and Eversley, pp. 73–5).

If psychological factors could thus serve to depress the rate of population growth either by delaying marriage or through the conscious control of births, we may assume that the converse was also possible. We may be sure that psychological factors were at work in the acceleration of growth in England in the last quarter of the eighteenth century. It was a period of impetuous economic development on all sides, of fresh opportunities for employment, with new facilities for housing and for the provision of domestic equipment. The propensity to marry would be at a maximum, and that there was a rise in the birth-rate, at least in towns, seems indisputable. In Nottingham the crude birth-rate, which had risen to 40·32 per thousand in 1770, reached the unprecedented height of 46·29 in 1790, but then fell back to 41·07 by 1800 (Chambers, 1960, p. 122). Coupled with high fertility was a marriage rate of 12 per thousand. Houses by the hundred were being built to serve the needs of a bourgeoning population and the double lure of living accommodation and high pay was irresistible. The birth-rate rose primarily as a reflection of the new age structure which a massive immigration of young country labour brought about, although it may be presumed that high marital fertility would also be in evidence in these propitious circumstances.

In view of its losses by migrations, it is all the more surprising that the eighteenth-century rural population showed such remarkable buoyancy. Birth-rates in the Nottinghamshire agricultural villages remained at over 30 per thousand while in the industrialized villages they rose to more than 35 per thousand (Chambers, 1957, p. 55). In the towns, the death-rate tended to rise to the level, and if anything above the level, that it reached in the early part of the century, so that those who looked to the birth-rate as the most important urban variable in the explosive period from 1790 have some foundation for this view. Whether the same can be said of the rural population is doubtful. The evidence points to a fall in the death-rate as being the most important factor, at least in the agricultural villages, and since they were by far the more numerous, their influence would be paramount at that time; but there is no doubt that fertility was well maintained, owing perhaps to the greater use of cottage labour and the relative decline of the numbers living in. The largest inquiry that has yet been attempted in this area of investigation is that of Dr Tranter who made a comparative examination of marital fertility for eight Bedfordshire parishes in the two periods of the last quarter of the seventeenth century and the third quarter of the eighteenth. He found only a slight tendency for the age of marriage to fall, perhaps only by one year, and for fertility rates of completed families to advance only by a fraction (1966, pp. 150–1, 174). For Colyton, Dr Wrigley found evidence of a marked fall in the age of marriage in the early nineteenth century, so that we may tentatively conclude that, if there was any substantial change in rural family size, it took place very late in the eighteenth century and more probably at the beginning of the nineteenth.

ILLEGITIMACY AND PRE-NUPTIAL CONCEPTIONS

If the Bedfordshire villages provide little evidence of a significant change in family size during the period of Dr Tranter's investigation, there is mounting evidence that change was taking place in two final aspects to which we must turn, namely the prevalence of illegitimacy and the growing proportion of pre-marital conceptions. The increase of illegitimacy towards the end of the eighteenth century is vouched for by all students of population history and is generally reflected in the records of the parishes so far examined. It has been suggested that bastardy rates may have risen from 5 per cent of all births to about 10 or more by the beginning of the nineteenth century (Glass and Eversley, p. 51). The actual record is considerably less than this, but the registering of bastardy may well have declined with the weakening of ecclesiastical control. It also appears that the recorded rate varied substantially from one region to another and from one period to another. It may well be that seventeenth-century parishes would show considerable variation according to the strictness or laxity of ecclesiastical control: under the stern eye of William Sampson the village of Clayworth had only a proportion of 1·9 per cent between 1676 and 1701, and

Ludlow's rate doubled from 3.8 per cent in 1590–1640 to 7.8 per cent between 1748–55 (Laslett, p. 134). Perhaps the exigencies of Poor Rates and the severity of Poor Law Officers also exercised an influence. In some parishes notorious mothers of bastards were ducked and whipped. Magistrates could be cruelly harsh to the mother; in 1729 three women in Nottingham were ordered to be whipped at the house of correction and then drawn in a cart down Stoney Street, High Pavement, Bridlesmith Gate, round the Malt Cross, then back to the workhouse where they were to be ducked. Country magistrates may have been more humane. There are examples of overseers and constables being bound over for such offences as removing a woman in her labour and dropping a sick woman in the highway. But there was still a tradition in south Nottinghamshire some years ago which I found on my rounds looking for parish account books, of 'knob-stick weddings', when reluctant fathers of bastard children were conducted to the altar between the church wardens, with upraised knob-sticks in case of an attempted get-away: and the high water mark of achievement on the part of a parish officer in any part of the country was to arrange a marriage between the harlot of his own village and the village idiot of the next. This was part of the England we have lost, for which Mr Laslett uttered such a moving requiem.

In the second half of the eighteenth century, the administration of bastardy became a matter of routine and the question of punishment seems to have been ignored. The relaxation of administrative sanctions reflected a growing incidence of recorded bastardy: in both Bedfordshire and Nottinghamshire villages the percentage of recorded cases rose from rather less than 1 per cent of the baptisms to over 4 per cent in the last quarter of the century (Chambers, 1957, p. 59: Tranter, 1966, p. 183), though it seems to have been a good deal higher in other areas.

A more significant reflection of the change in the moral climate is the increase in the proportion of pre-nuptial conceptions. This can be ascertained by calculating the interval between the date of marriage of the parents and that of the baptism of the first child. But since the interval between births and baptisms varied from place to place and period to period, no rule of universal application can be laid down for calculations of this kind, and local conditions have to be taken into account. For instance Dr Tranter in his investigation of Bedfordshire villages found that the mean interval between birth and baptism lengthened from 13 days in 1740–50 to 87 days by 1801–12 (1966, pp. 158–9). For this reason he has regarded all baptisms that were registered less than nine months after the date of marriage as having been conceived before the union with the following results (1966, p. 244):

TABLE 5

Pre-nuptial Conceptions in Bedfordshire, 1670–1790
(per cent)

1670–80	1690–1700	1720–30	1740–50	1765–75	1785–1790
12	11	22	35	35	40

It is difficult to escape the conclusion that by the second half of the eighteenth century, among the factors that influenced fertility we must include the phenomenon of a changed moral attitude.

We are left with the general conclusion that the history of fertility in pre-industrial England went through a series of changes reflecting both the physical circumstances and the moral attitudes of the time. The onslaught of plague in the fourteenth century and again in the case of Colyton in 1646 was followed by a fall in fertility of considerable duration reflecting, it would seem, psychological as well as biological factors. Each instance was followed by a period of recovery, but the long-term sequel in the two cases was very different. Wheras the recovery of the sixteenth century was followed by a further setback in the seventeenth, that of the eighteenth century was the prelude to an acceleration amounting to a veritable population explosion in the last decade of the century. Evidently new factors were at work. One was the factor of greater confidence in the opportunities now being offered, and another a relaxation in the traditional moral code, finding a reflection in rising fertility especially in the last decade of the century. Yet, more important than either was the factor of the death-rate, which in the two earlier periods of recovery had reasserted itself; in the eighteenth century the death-rate failed to catch up with the birth-rate. The gap between them was never closed; instead it widened, and in falling, the death-rate brought a new age structure into being. Perhaps after all, it is to the death-rate that we must look if we are to find the deciding factor in the race between baptisms and burials, between the number of babies brought to the font and bodies to the graveyard. For the first time in the history of man the microbiological world was unable to hold in check the forces of human fecundity, and we shall consider this apocalyptic turn of affairs in the next chapter.

4

The Chances of Life and the Autonomous Death-rate

FROM the evidence so far on population change, the abiding impression is one of fluctuations in which the responsiveness of marriage and fertility to changing circumstances played an important part. The indirect check propounded by Malthus appears to have operated in the first instance through changes in the age of marriage; and there is an increasing tendency among students of demography to infer that it operated also within marriage. It would seem that these responses to external circumstances are to be found throughout the entire social spectrum of which we have record, from Mr Hollingsworth's dukes to Dr Wrigley's villagers of Colyton; and it also appears that the relative incidence of this responsiveness was affected to some extent by social status, the higher the social status the larger the family and the higher the recorded fertility.

It would be unrealistic to conclude from this that the entire responsibility for the differential prudential check on the size of the family operated only on the side of the birth-rate. Was nothing done via the death-rate in the struggle to keep numbers under social control? Wrigley has reminded us that

the parish register . . . carries no clues as to the methods of family limitation used. These may never be known with certainty, but it is likely that there was scope for the quiet disposal outside the ecclesiastical purview of abortions, and, indeed, of the victims of infanticide . . . The early hours of a child's life provide many occasions when it is easy to follow the maxim that 'thou shalt not kill but needst not strive officiously to keep alive' (1966, p. 105).

It is with this in mind that Professor Krause has written, 'the usually cited infant death-rates greatly exaggerate pre-industrial

infant mortality, especially among infants born to families which
wanted to keep them alive' (1959, p. 177). To what extent recorded burials were inflated by names that should or need not
have been there is impossible to say, but if we could add to that
those who had no name at all and passed out of the world as
surreptitiously as they came in, the proportion would be substantial. Something is known of this aspect of infant mortality from
the grim records of London. Rickman calculated the London
death-rate on the assumption that one-third of the deaths escaped
registration, and of this a considerable proportion must be regarded as the direct or indirect result of human agency. Exposure
in the streets, desertion by parents, and a deliberate destruction
of infant life by parish authorities were everyday occurrences in
London, perhaps especially in the first half of the eighteenth
century. Dr J. C. Cox in his classic study of parish registers shows
that the practice of sending out children from London and other
large towns to nurseries in the country goes back to Elizabethan
times, and from the large incidence of burials among them he
concludes this must be regarded as a form of baby-farming. Again,
alongside the 240 foundlings whose names are found in the
register of the Temple in the eighteenth century there are 170
burials. It is interesting to note that to nearly all of them the
surname Temple or Templer is assigned (pp. 67–8). Many other
examples of surnames derived from the place in which a foundling
was taken up could be given, but none quite so remarkable as
that recorded in the register for St Helen's, Bishopsgate, in 1612—
'Job Rakt-out-of the Asshes, being borne the last day of August
in the lane going to Sir John Spencer's back gate and there laide
in a heape of old cold asshes, was baptized the first daye of
September following, and dyed the next day after' (Cox, p. 64).
It is known, too, that in 1715, when the House of Commons set
up a committee on the care of the poor in the parish of St Martin
in the Fields, they found that 900 of the 1,200 babies born every
year in the parish died, many of them being exposed or over-laid
by women described as nurses. The evidence of Thomas Coram
is quite explicit on the point. 'No expedient has yet been found
out', he wrote in 1739,

for preventing the murder of poor miserable infants at their birth, or
suppressing the inhuman custom of exposing newly-born infants to
perish in the streets; or the putting of such unhappy foundlings to

wicked and barbarous nurses, who undertake to bring them up for a small and trifling sum of money [and] do often suffer them to starve for want of due sustenance and care (George, p. 56).

Appalled at the sight of children exposed and dead in the streets of London, he worked for seventeen years to establish the Foundling Hospital and by 1745 one wing of the building was in use. In 1756 it received government help on condition that its doors were open to all who might apply. Its gates were thereupon besieged by parents not only from London but from the country outside. The children were entrusted to carriers and wagoners, even vagrants. Untold numbers, it is said, died on the way, and the site of the hospital was turned into a burial ground. During a short-lived period of three years and ten months of wholesale admissions, 14,000 children were taken in of whom only 4,500 lived to be apprenticed. Under the influence of an enlightened body of governors of whom Josiah Hanway was one, the death-rate was reduced after 1760 to 1 in 4 and by the end of the century it was less than 1 in 6. At the same time, steps were taken to check the appalling waste of life in workhouses; out of 291 children taken in by 11 workhouses in 1763, Hanway reported that 256—94 per cent—were dead by the end of 1765. It says something for the changing attitudes of the age that this remarkable man was able within two years to steer an Act through Parliament which put a stop to this terrible scandal. By the Act of 1767, all parish children under six were to be sent out of London to be nursed, and nurses were to have a reward of 10 shillings for every child sent to them under nine months whom they successfully reared (George, pp. 56–9). For the first time in our history, the State was beginning to spend money on the saving of life, and though in numerical terms the saving was no doubt marginal, it is a sign of the times that must not be overlooked. It also had the effect of providing a source of child labour to the cotton mills in the second half of the century and to that extent made a direct contribution to the recruitment of the labour force for the Industrial Revolution.

How large a factor private and institutional infanticide was, we shall never know: but we can be sure that, compared to the natural causes which hovered over them from the moment of birth, death by direct or indirect human agency was of minor significance, a mere eddy on the tide of mortality that swept away

the generations, sometimes, and in some places, with such speed
that they were scarcely given time to replace themselves. Marriages
were frequently broken by the death of one or other of the
parents. Remarriages were very frequent and the average of
recorded baptisms per marriage was rarely more than 5. In
Colyton the average of all marriages between 1560 and 1629 was
just over 4. This is a dangerously low level when the expectation
of life at birth is low; if it falls below 24 it could, indeed, represent the point at which the population was no longer replacing
itself. In many villages this may very well have happened from
time to time. We have heard a great deal about lost villages
and the replacement of peasants by sheep. We might also consider the demographic argument that owing to the high death-rate
and low expectation of life in some of these villages, the replacement rate had fallen to less than unity. Many of them are known
to have been situated on high, cold soils, where conditions of life
may have tilted the balance in the struggle for survival without
the assistance of the enclosing landlord.

That such a situation was by no means impossible has been
made abundantly clear in the study mentioned earlier by Professor
Thrupp of the replacement rate in a number of Lincolnshire
villages in the century after the Black Death. For the first time
we are given a clue to the problem of the demographic depression
that settled on England in the period 1350–1450 when resources
per head were higher than ever before in pre-industrial English
society. Probably the death-rate was rising before the onset of the
plague; and a static level may have been reached, it is thought,
from about the end of the thirteenth century. Whether the population was making anything of a recovery after the famines of
1315–17 it is impossible to say, for all we know for certain is that
when the plague struck the effect was devastating; and it continued through successive attacks in 1348–9, 1360–1, 1369, and
1375, by which time the population had probably been reduced
by up to half. It might be expected that there would be a surge
of fertility that would quickly replace the lost numbers, but
Thrupp has shown that this was not the case. She gives examples
of villages where male replacement rates varied up to 1·8 before
the epidemic struck, whereas during the epidemic period the
replacement rate for Hinderclay was no more than 0·53 for the
1340s and '50s (pp. 106–8). After the second pandemic of 1361

the replacement rate was even lower and subsequently matters
were worse still: 'In Northwold, Norfolk, the picture between
1414 and 1459 was truly shocking,' she writes. Of 23 cases, 11
(47 per cent) had no sons and 10 died childless (pp. 110–11). By
the third quarter of the fifteenth century, however, there occurred
an upward trend of marriage and births which resulted in higher
replacement rates. An examination of the wills of the Arch-
deaconry of Essex shows that between 1420 and 1435 the number
of sons mentioned per testator was 0·54; in the period 1477–9
the number rose to 0·7 and between 1480 and 1492 it was 1·18
(p. 115). The pattern is one of a rising marriage rate due to
better chances of survival and of a markedly better survival of
male children from the 1470s.

How do we account for the demographic cloud that had hung
over England in the century following the Black Death? It is
tempting to assume that the pandemic of 1389 continued to run
its course in the fifteenth and to thin the ranks of survivors and
their offspring. Dr Bean, however, has assembled evidence to show
that the subsequent outbreaks were too local and sporadic in their
incidence to have this effect, and has concluded, therefore, that
since the only known cause that could have kept the rate of
growth down did not operate, the rate could not have gone down
but may even have gone up! (p. 435). In the face of Thrupp's
evidence, this hypothesis can hardly be entertained: the stagnation
seems to be an incontrovertible fact. Like Bean, however, Thrupp
acquits the Great Plague of responsibility for it. 'Although in the
late fourteenth century and at certain points later, plague must
have radically altered the age structure of the population . . . it
is converting history into grand opera to make the macabre
character of the plague responsible for the long sluggishness of
replacement rates in the fifteenth century' (pp. 117–18). If, then,
the cause was not the plague, what was it? We have already
mentioned Dr Creighton's suggestion that plague left a legacy
of sterility in the surviving women. Thrupp does not consider
this; but she speaks instead of 'bacterial and viral mutation' and
considers that historians should be prepared to accept this as a
factor in the situation. 'New types of infection', she says, 'are
always dangerous, and travel and communication are their best
friends.' Her conclusion is, therefore, that 'the period from 1349
to the 1470s, if it was a Golden Age, was the golden age of

bacteria', and this, she suggests, was associated with a desire to escape the responsibilities of marriage, a psychological or, as she puts it, a 'cultural explanation' of the continued stagnation of population (pp. 117–18).

We are now brought face to face with the irrevocable fact which historians have been loath to recognize, the fact of the autonomous death-rate, the death-rate which could override countervailing influences, such as low prices, an abundance of free land, a shortage of labour, and rising real wages.

The historical significance of the fortuitous element in the death-rate was commented on more than twenty years ago by John Saltmarsh in his paper on 'Plague and Economic Decline in England in the later Middle Ages', in which the depredations of the black rat (*Rattus rattus*) and the brown rat (*Rattus norvegicus*) were brought to the notice of economic historians as a factor in long-term economic as well as demographic change.

It closes with an important statement which is worth repeating:

The great disaster of the Black Death has distracted the attention of historians from the later and lesser epidemics of plague; but these, in their cumulative effect, may well explain more in English history than the Black Death itself . . . it is necessary to bear in mind that epidemic disease has more power over human life than famine, flood or tempest, let alone the march of armies or the policy of kings (pp. 40–1).

In the twenty years since this article was written enough evidence has accumulated to justify a reopening of the discussion.

THE PLAGUE

The first attack in 1348 is evidently an example of the impact of disease *per se* without a preliminary softening up by famine, flood, or war. Certainly the preceding century was a period of population pressure and therefore undernourishment, but it may be presumed that the terrible crisis of 1315–17, which was characterized by every horror of famine, including cannibalism, had somewhat relieved the pressure. It had also been accompanied by dysentery through the eating of corrupt food and there were complaints of 'putrid sore throats'; but apart from the bad harvest of 1332, the intervening period between these calamities and the Black Death seems to have been unmarked by famine or pestilence. Creighton, indeed, speaks of 'a long succession of cheap years, covering the interval to the next great event in the annals of pestilence . . . the arrival of the Black Death' (i. 49).

What, then, is the explanation of the appalling catastrophe that fell upon Britain in August 1348? Eminent authorities treat it as a form of Malthusian nemesis falling upon the population of Europe after the frenetic expansion of the thirteenth century. Slicher Van Bath is very specific. He says, 'Prolonged malnutrition heightens the chance of epidemics breaking out; infectious diseases take a much heavier toll. This is the explanation of the havoc wrought by the Black Death and other epidemics of the fourteenth century' (p. 84). But the infectious diseases did not break out until 1348, long after the peak of the Malthusian subsistence crisis had been passed; and the subsequent epidemics occurred when prices were falling and land supply was in excess of demand. Why invoke Malthus to explain these disasters? Would it not be more sensible to regard the Black Death and its subsequent manifestations as crises of public health essentially biological in character reflecting the concentration of animal infection of explosive force—not directly related to problems of subsistence, but stemming from an epizootic crisis among the rodent population which carried the infection? It was known by the end of 1346, Mr Ziegler tells us, that a plague of unparalleled fury was raging in the East; it had reached India where whole provinces had been laid waste, but 'it does not seem to have occurred to anyone that the plague would strike at Europe' (p. 15). Why should it? Such an occurrence was unheard of; it was unique and quite out of character with any epidemic with which man had had experience. Famine was a commonplace; so was disease. But this was something new.

Strictly speaking, the Black Death, as it came later to be called (probably to distinguish it from the Great Plague of London), is not a human disease at all. It is an example—one of many— of the transference of disease bacilli from an infected animal as a result of which the human victim may (but need not) become a carrier, at which point it becomes a human disease, especially if it takes the pneumonic form. It is thus the result of special circumstances which involve the interaction of the plague bacillus (*Pasteurella pestis*), the flea that carries it (*Xenopsylla cheopis*), and the rodent, usually the rat, which is itself infected by it. When the bacillus is taken from an infected animal it multiplies

D

in the flea's stomach and in favourable conditions will increase so fast as to obstruct the gullet of the flea, with the result that the blood sucked in from the next host is regurgitated back into the victim's blood-stream as it would be from the action of a hypodermic syringe, thus carrying with it some of the plague bacilli. This is usually followed by a high fever and the appearance of buboes in the groin and armpits and small black pustules on the skin. The parasite may attack the lungs, which results in the far more deadly pneumonic plague and the spread of the infection through breathing infected air. There is also a third and far more rare variety, the septicaemic plague which is characterized by concentration of baccilli in the blood-stream so great that there is no time for buboes to form and the victim can die within a few hours. The plague flea—*Xenopsylla cheopis*—may be carried in the interstices of bales of cloth as at Eyam in 1665 or Marseilles in 1720, in which case the initial onslaught might be expected to be more voracious for the enforced period of starvation by the plague flea during transit.

A further characteristic of the bubonic plague is that it prefers to infest the indoor black rat (*Rattus rattus*)—'the tough, nimble by nature vagabond black rat'—a migration of which from Central Asia may have been the initiatory agency of the great pandemic. Why it attacked with such overwhelming violence is still a mystery, but the argument that it was a Malthusian nemesis of the over-expansion of the century 1150–1250 leaves out the important fact that it was an Oriental as much as a Western phenomenon, and wholly Oriental in origin.

As to its virulence, it is perhaps sufficient to refer to the rough proportions of the English population that, according to Professor Russell's estimates, were swept away in the successive waves of pestilence between 1348 and 1375. Total mortality is put at 23·6 per cent for 1348–50, 18·7 per cent for 1360–1, 13·0 per cent for 1369, and 11·6 per cent for 1374. After deducting 'normal' mortality, the plague is calculated to have accounted for 16·6, 12·7, 10·0, and 8·6 per cent of the population respectively, and the indications are that the English population of 1377 was 40 per cent down on the 1348 level (p. 263).

In the following century there were five national outbreaks—1407, 1413, 1434, 1439, 1464—and numerous local outbreaks, which included a high proportion confined to London or to other urban centres. Dr Bean, to whom we are indebted for this information, infers that they were mainly bubonic in character and lacked the fierce infective powers of the pneumonic variety; otherwise the habit that had developed of fleeing to the country would have had effect of spreading the infection (pp. 430–2).

The later history of the plague in England repeats the experience of sporadic and local outbreaks of the fifteenth century with especially severe attacks in 1563, 1593, 1597, 1603, 1608–10, 1625, 1636, and 1665. The mortality of the so-called Great Plague of London of 1665 was probably not greatly in excess, if at all, of that of 1625 which claimed more than 40,000 victims in London alone (i.e. one-eighth of the population), and caused a slump in trade; and there is some reason to think that the population of London was actually lower in 1631 than in 1603, though the gaps were eventually made up by a great rise in baptisms and still more by the continued influx of people from the country. Table 6 is eloquent of the buoyancy of population and also of the deadly seasonality of the plague (Creighton, i. 660):

TABLE 6

Plague Mortality in London

Crises	Population of London	London deaths	Plague deaths	Highest in a week	Worst weeks
1603	250,000	42,940	33,347	3,385	25 Aug.–1 Sept.
1625	320,000	63,001	41,313	5,205	11–18 Aug.
1665	460,000	97,306	68,596	8,297	12–19 Sept.

Within two years after the catastrophe of 1665, the plague disappeared; its last significant appearance was in Nottingham and Newark in 1667. It reappeared on the continent of Europe in the terrible Marseilles outbreak of 1720–2, after which it never again reached epidemic proportions in Western Europe.

THE PROBLEM OF IMMUNITY

The disappearance of the plague is one of the greatest puzzles of epidemiological history. It has been attributed to the victory of the brown rat (*Rattus norvegicus*), which tends to shun human habitation, over the black rat, which loves the haunts of men. But when did this victory take place? The brown rat had been known in Western Europe since Roman times and the great swarming over the Volga, which may have heralded its victory, did not occur until 1727. The immunity of Britain from 1665 until the time that the brown rat had established its ascendancy still has to be accounted for. The Great Fire, followed by the rebuilding of London, would play its part and the substitution of brick and tile for stud and mud and thatch which was taking place at an accelerating pace throughout the country was perhaps more important.

But something more fundamental may have been involved. Modern evidence suggests that in some circumstances, following an intense and prolonged epizootic, the rats themselves can build up a 'marked rise in resistance to infection' (Hirst, p. 258); while we have already noticed the same author's suggestion (p. 338) that the change in the rat species must be associated with a change in flea species to account for the relative immunity from plague in modern times. These are comforting thoughts in view of the fact that the black rat has made something of a comeback in its old haunts in London, and its ability to climb over roofs and along overhead telephone cables renders our modern tall buildings especially vulnerable to its depredations. Moreover, it is still unknown why the bacillus of plague suddenly becomes virulent: nor is it understood why its ravages in the seventeenth century were reinforced by other forms of infection, especially smallpox, typhus, ague, and various unidentifiable forms of fevers. Perhaps we should take into account the possibility that the exchange of infectious diseases between continents as a result of European navigation in the sixteenth century had some responsibility for the increase of death-rates everywhere in the following century.

As a crowning example of the fortuitous nature of this scourge of civilization everywhere, it may be of value to cite the last visitation of the bubonic plague to Western Europe in the early eighteenth century. After devastating Eastern Europe between 1709 and 1712, it seems to have 'exhausted its power of diffusion' when it reached Bavaria, and was unable to penetrate any further. To the people of Western Europe 'it must have seemed', says Professor Helleiner, 'as if their countries had acquired some sort of immunity'. But in 1720 they were given a further reminder of the fearful nature of the threat that still hung over them: in that year the plague killed 40,000 people in Marseilles out of 90,000; one-third of the inhabitants of Aix-en-Provence, Martigues, and Saint-Remy as well as half of Toulon, Auriol, and Berre and three-quarters of Arles and La Valetta; it caused the Pope to stop up six of the sixteen gates of Rome to facilitate inspection of travellers and stimulated a boom in English cloth in preference to cloth from the infected towns of France. And that was the end; the plague inexplicably failed to spread beyond the borders of Provence and by August 1721 it was all over (Glass and Eversley, p. 81).

I think it is arguable that random biological causes operating in successive onslaughts on an already high death-rate were so powerful through to the middle of the eighteenth century that they could initiate long waves of demographic depression independently of available *per capita* resources; and that conversely the absence of such biological factors could result in lowering the death-rate and in inducing a population rise to the point at which, on occasion, direct Malthusian checks might begin to operate, as for instance in the boom of population in the century before the Black Death. In other words, it can be argued that the long-term trend in population change was non-economic in origin. Once a trend had declared itself, it became an economic factor of great importance through its influence on market forces of supply and demand both of labour and goods, and these in their turn influenced the population trend through their effect on the provision of employment opportunities and so on nuptiality and natality.

EPIDEMICS AND HARVESTS

Accordingly, the relative importance of epidemics and harvests in influencing population change is worthy of closer study. As a result of the development of local and regional studies the principle of the primacy of food supply in determining population change has come under closer scrutiny by historians, and they are encouraged in their more critical attitude by the pronouncements of some of their colleagues in the field of medical therapy. Professor Hare, for instance, writes, 'although it is frequently stated that both starvation and shortage of vitamins render the host abnormally susceptible to infection, there is actually very little evidence that such is the case'; and also queries the view that a deficient diet would render the antibody-forming apparatus unable to carry out its functions properly (p. 107). If this is correct, we may conclude that an epidemic might accompany a food crisis and perform its role of pruning the population, or it might not; the effect of the food crisis might be confined to exacerbating the impact of endemic causes of ill-health such as pneumonia, tuberculosis, and the common cold, with some repercussions on the death-rate no doubt, but the effect would be essentially short-term and the level of population would soon be restored. As the 'harvest sensitive' segment of the population shrank with the improvement of agriculture and transport, the impact of harvest crises would be less marked while the impact of epidemics would become relatively greater. This, as we shall see later, seems to have been the case in the late seventeenth century; but as the factors making for the taming of epidemic power made themselves felt in the second half of the eighteenth century, the factor of food shortage as measured by prices appears once more to have assumed a relative primacy as a short-time regulator of population.

It is interesting to note that the view regarding the relatively minor effect of hunger upon the death-rate has a long and highly respectable ancestry. As early as 1778, the distinguished writer on French population, Mortyon, 'denied the influence of dearth upon mortality' (Vincent, p. 59). This, by implication, would leave epidemic disease as the senior partner in this dual alliance of demographic regulators; but the opposite view, soon to be propounded with such force by Malthus in his *Essay on the Principle of Population* (1798), prevailed. Yet Mr Udny Ule has pointed out, Creighton tried but frequently failed to establish a connection between the incidence of fevers during the early part of the nineteenth century with periods of economic depression (p. 28); and examples of the same difficulties could easily be given in his treatment of so-called 'famine epidemics' in Volume I in which the direct relationship between famine and epidemics can be seen to break down again and again.

More recently, the Swedish historian Professor Heckscher, although a convinced Malthusian, had to admit in his *Economic History of Sweden* (p. 136) that while mortality rates showed periodicity of from five to six years from peak to peak, that of prices was much less regular. As I have pointed out elsewhere (Chambers, 1957, p. 27), the Nottingham historian Dr Deering would have had no difficulty in accepting a high mortality every five to six years, which he attributed to the smallpox cycle, but he would not have been able to share Heckscher's surprise at its failure to conform to the fluctuation of the harvest.

The various inconsistencies in Heckscher's account have been examined at length by his fellow countryman Gustav Utterström, who has now presented a more flexible view of the relationship between environmental circumstances and mortality which would probably be accepted by most students of the subject. 'Some investigators', he writes,

following a Malthusian model, have regarded epidemics by and large simply as the instrument which held population at the level determined by the means of subsistence. Of course, it is clear that there were always certain contagious diseases in progress and that deaths from such epidemics usually rose when the food situation became critical. But this by no means precludes that diseases which were given a common name could appear in different forms and with varying degrees of fatality irrespective of the food supply. Furthermore, certain diseases were not endemic but broke out at irregular intervals, e.g. the plague, cholera, ague. . . . There were times in Sweden during the eighteenth century when mortality rose only slightly despite serious crop failures; there are also examples of good harvests followed by a steep rise in mortality (Glass and Eversley, pp. 544–5).

Epidemics, also, according to the Malthusian analysis, should perform the role of weeding out the physically weak, but Utterström points out that this process would be influenced by the factor of immunity which might be conferred on the weak as well as the strong. Again, the apparent connection between a bad harvest and an epidemic might consist more in the release of a swarm of infected beggars rather than in initiating the epidemic itself; and similarly a flood might set off a migration of infected rats to higher ground or a late harvest might induce an infestation of rats because of the food left on the ground; while there is always the baffling problem of seasonality which is primarily a biological problem and only marginally explicable in terms of food supply. There is good reason to think, too, that the factor of immunity might affect the age distribution of those at risk, as seems to have happened in the case of smallpox, and there seems no doubt that social structure influenced the infectivity of the mysterious epidemic of the English Sweat.

It is one of the advantages of the local studies upon which some of us have been lately engaged that they provide opportunity for examining the relative importance of harvests or epidemics on mortality more closely than has hitherto been possible. A brief review of this evidence on the basis of the various examples of regional studies that have been made will now be attempted. It will take the form, first, of an impressionistic account of the sequence of harvests as indicated by prices and the fluctuation of mortality as recorded in parish registers; this will then be followed by a more rigorous analysis in one geographical area where the necessary data happen to be available. To begin with the impressionistic account of the relation of prices and mortality; it will be remembered that Professor Hoskins raised this question in a broadcast published in *The Listener* (1964). He pointed out how unevenly the plague struck his Devon villages in 1546–7, not merely between villages, but between families. In one village, nearly half the deaths occurred in 8 per cent of the families. Moreover certain parishes and certain families escaped altogether, and he goes on, 'if malnutrition had been an aggravating cause of plague, why not generally instead of just here and there? It will be difficult to establish any correlation between malnutrition and mortality from plague' (pp. 1004–5). It is doubtful, however, whether the same could be said of town populations where the poor tended to make closer contact and therefore ran more risk from infection.

To take another example of a village population, it will be remembered that Mr Laslett in his book *The World We Have Lost* was puzzled to find so little correlation between the level of infant mortality at Clayworth and the price index of wheat between 1680 and 1703 (pp. 126–7).

TABLE 7

Registered Infant Mortality at Clayworth, Notts

Infant deaths per thousand				
1680–2	385	Price Index 1676–85	64·5	(1682–77·0)
1683–5	300			
1686–8	350			
1689–91	242	Price Index 1686–96	53·4	(1690–43·7)
1692–4	185			
1695–7	168			
1698–1700	117	Price Index 1696–1701	68·4	(1698–103·5)

He concludes, quite rightly, that nothing can be made of the vague tendency of the level of local cereal prices to vary with numbers of babies dying. Certainly nothing can; but a great deal could have been made of the far-from-vague tendency of the number of deaths to vary with the course of the terrible epidemic that was sweeping through the Midland counties at this time. The height of the epidemic occurred between 1678 and 1681 when, in twenty-six Nottinghamshire villages, burials reached an annual aggregate of over 400 and baptisms were below 300. The population of these villages must have been cut down by almost 400 in these three years (Chambers, 1957, pp. 28, 35). Mr Laslett's price index averaged 64·5 in 1676–85, attaining 77 in 1682; but this was by no means the highest figure in the series. Between 1696 and 1701 the index was 68·4 and in 1698 it actually reached 103·5; yet in this period births outstripped deaths by the widest margin for fifty years. By confessing his bewilderment at the strange behaviour of the death-rate in Clayworth in the early 1680s, Mr Laslett is inadvertently drawing attention to a striking example of the fortuitous element in the death-rate at that time: it was more obedient to disease than to famine prices.

What was the nature of the disease(s) that had such disastrous effects on the Nottinghamshire villages? Creighton identifies the sickness of 1678–81 as epidemic intermittent ague, or, 'the years of the aguish epidemic constitution'. It gave rise to some macabre forms of humour among its victims, who called it the New Acquaintance or, in Derbyshire, the New Delight (ii. 332–5). In 1685–6 there followed a great epidemic of continued fever, or typhus, 'different from any that had prevailed for seven years before', and attributed by Dr Sydenham to 'some secret and recondite change in the bowels of the earth pervading the whole atmosphere, or some influence of the celestial bodies' (ii. 22–3). Creighton specifically notes that it had 'slight relation to famine or scarcity', although there had been an intense frost in the winter of 1683–4 followed by drought and another 'long and cruel frost' in 1684–5 (ii. 23). The association of high mortality with severe and prolonged cold over two seasons may well be significant, more perhaps in prolonging than in initiating the crisis.

But if the years 1679–86 provide an example of epidemics without the accompanying famine, the next decade provides the opposite: famine without disease. The notorious 'seven ill years' (1692–9) which worked such havoc in Scotland do not seem to be reflected in the mortality of Nottinghamshire villages nor, indeed, in the country generally to the extent that might have been expected.

They appear, on the contrary, to be years of substantial surplus of baptisms over burials (Chambers, 1957, pp. 28, 35). The fact that in Scotland these bad harvests loosed a swarm of beggars who roamed the countryside in search of food does not seem to have brought infection beyond the northern counties of England, and we may take this as a significant example of the failure of very severe distress to initiate high mortality unless it was accompanied by appropriate bacterial pre-conditions.

The famine of 1710, when wheat rose to 80 shillings a quarter, is perhaps the most remarkable example of all in its failure to conform to Malthusian expectations. 'Famine' is not too hard a word to describe the conditions of that terrible year. Moreover it was widespread, affecting the continent of Europe as well as England, thus cutting off the possibility of supply from abroad. Yet mortality levels in the Nottinghamshire villages were only marginally higher than usual, though the marriages sank to their lowest ever. The explanation seems to be that these years were spoken of by the doctors favourably: 'It was a time when there was a great lull in smallpox and perhaps fevers.' It is significant, too, that Dr Short's study of parish registers shows that in regard to excess of deaths over births 'these years are as little conspicuous as any' (Chambers, 1957, pp. 25–6).

From this time the impact of epidemics appears to take on a grimmer aspect. The following forty years were a period of generally good harvests and, for a large part of the period, phenomenally low prices, but there were breaks in the sequence, especially in 1728–9 and 1740–1, when high prices were accompanied by fierce epidemics resulting in very high mortality. In 1728 wheat reached 54 shillings a quarter and 47 shillings in 1729 despite a net import of grain: medical writers talked of a new pathological phenomenon which they described as relapsing or putrid fever, which may have been a variety of typhus. No doubt influenza played a part and also smallpox, though the evidence for this is not decisive. It was especially severe on the poor and, as noted above, according to Dr Hilary of Ripon, 'it almost stripped many of the little country towns and villages of their people all over the northern part of the kingdom'. 'I observed', he writes, 'that very few of the richer people who used a generous way of living and were not exposed to the inclemencies of the weather, were seized with any of these diseases at the time' (Chambers, 1957, p. 29). Here we have the deadly combination of bad weather, high but not famine prices, and the agents of virulent disease aided by primitive medical practice with results that justify the view that this decade saw an actual net decline of population.

The years 1740–1 were, if anything, somewhat worse, at least among the town population. The price of wheat in 1740 was little more than half it had been in 1709–10, i.e. 45 shillings as against 80 shillings—but the results were catastrophic, and in Nottingham 1 in 13 of the inhabitants died, that is, a death-rate of over 70 per thousand (Chambers, 1957, p. 30; 1960, p. 110). Again we are seeing an example of the fearful effects of disease, probably part of the typhus wave that was sweeping over Europe, on a population suffering from the effects of two bad harvests and the unheard-of frost in 1739–40, so severe, we are told, that 'many hens and ducks and even cattle in their stalls died of cold'. It should be remembered that Nottingham was a prosperous town in good communication with sources of supply from the fertile lands of the Vale of Trent, and it may be that prolonged cold rather than food supply was the deciding factor that raised the power of disease to the second highest level of the century.

Roughly half-way between these two attacks there was one of a different character. It was unquestionably an outbreak of smallpox, and may be associated with the excessively wet summer of 1736 which damaged the hay and corn crops of the low-lying areas and caused the price of wheat to rise to 34 shillings. This is far from a famine price, but in combination with the return of the smallpox cycle it was sufficient to raise mortality to epidemic levels (Chambers, 1957, p. 25). Again it seemed to be the state of the weather rather than the deficiency of food supply that provided the external stimulus to this disastrous attack. But there seems no doubt that we have here an example of smallpox of a very virulent kind, recognized as such by the local doctor and accepted as part of the quinquennial cycle to which the town had become accustomed.

From these examples, taken from a single region (the Vale of Trent), it would appear that about 1720 there was a switch from the relatively low levels of mortality ruling for the previous thirty years (in spite of some violent fluctuations of prices) to a period of exceptionally high mortality under the impact of deadly forms of infection—in particular typhus and smallpox—with high prices and bad weather playing supporting roles on all three occasions cited. Whether this Nottinghamshire pattern can be regarded as a guide to the demographic situation of the country as a whole remains an open question, but evidence can be drawn from three other inquiries which go some way to support such a claim. Dr Eversley's Worcestershire villages exhibited low burial rates between 1705 and 1714 ; they rose by 20 per cent between 1720 and 1724, and between 1725 and 1729 by 100 per cent (a death-rate of over 65 per thousand); they were evidently enduring a visitation of a peculiarly deadly kind, as in the Nottinghamshire villages (Glass and Eversley, p. 408). Mrs Sogner's study of Shropshire villages provides a pattern so closely akin to that of Nottinghamshire that at a superficial glance it might be mistaken for it. There is, however, a more rigorous test than any of these to be taken into account. It rests upon the exhaustive and much neglected study of epidemics in Exeter by Mr R. Pickard made more than twenty years ago together with the analysis of harvests and wheat prices compiled by Professor Hoskins (1968) for the country as a whole and for the West Country in particular on the basis of the Exeter wheat prices of Lord Beveridge. By setting these side by side we have as good a test of the relationship of the two variables as can be devised in the absence of more detailed local studies.

Pickard himself distinguishes seven epidemic years between 1664 and 1680 of which three (1668, 1677, 1678) can be associated with deficient harvests, and four with average harvests. The decade 1681–90 has the remarkable record of four epidemic years of which *all* were associated with 'good or even abundant harvests'; while the decade 1691–1700, including the 'seven ill years', is described by Pickard as 'a comparatively healthy period' except for 1695 when there was a terrible outbreak of fever in Somerset and Devon. This, it is interesting to note, was preceded by an abundant harvest in the west, while 1695 itself was classed as average. Of the other years of this remarkable decade, three harvests were bad, two were classed as dearths, three were average and only one was good. Yet it was not regarded as an unhealthy period (Pickard, p. 61; Hoskins (1968), pp. 29–30). This example can hardly give comfort to those who insist on finding a significant correlation between high prices and high mortality.

The following decade, like its two predecessors, confirms the experience of the Midlands. The years 1709–10 were both described

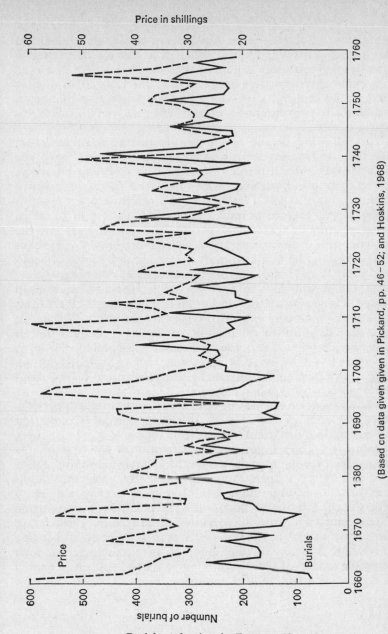

Price in shillings

Number of burials

Price

Burials

(Based on data given given in Pickard, pp. 46–52; and Hoskins, 1968)

FIG. 2: Burials and prices in Exeter, 1660–1760

as 'dearths', i.e. famine years, but Pickard records no evidence of excessive mortality for Exeter, although in this case mortality in 1711 was comparatively high. On the other hand 1716 and 1719 were epidemic years with average to good harvests and, as in most parts of the country, 1729 was a bad mortality year in Exeter, though the harvest itself was 'average' (Pickard, pp. 62-3; Hoskins (1968), p. 30).

The following decade was generally one of high mortality although the harvests were average to good. But in 1739 the sequence was broken; prices rose to 23·6 per cent above normal, and in 1740 to 50·5 per cent, whilst in Exeter in 1741 the deaths attained 1 in 19, and in Tiverton, 1 in 12 (Pickard, p. 64; Hoskins (1968), p. 31). Thus in general, the epidemic pattern of the West Country tends to reflect that of the Midland villages, but the existence of the Beveridge prices series reproduced by Hoskins makes possible the more rigorous examination to which I would now like to turn. Figure 2 sets out the raw data in a simple graphical form, and it will be seen that no simple, obvious relationship existed between fluctuations in burials and in prices. This confirms the scepticism already expressed regarding the effects of harvests upon mortality; but by calculating correlation coefficients we can go further. In point of fact, the coefficient for the period 1661–1759 as a whole is − 0·287 (notably, an *inverse*, although slight, relationship), whilst lagging the burials by one year or two years behind prices yields − 0·299 and − 0·077.

The relationship can also be investigated over three sub-periods: 1661–1715, 1716–39, and 1740–59. In this approach it is found that the correlation coefficients move from *minus* 0·362 (1661–1715 to *minus* 0·273 (1716–39) and then to + 0·353 for 1740–59 (or + 0·244 for 1740–99; the analysis has been carried beyond the date at which Figure 2 concludes). Since none of these correlation coefficients is strikingly high, I think we may infer that down to 1715 the chief factor in fluctuations in mortality was epidemic disease, which appears to have had no direct (positive) association with food shortage. In the years after 1740, since (modest) positive correlation is observed, the influence of subsistence was now becoming somewhat more significant as that of epidemics tended to decline, as a regulator of mortality.

FACTORS MAKING FOR THE DECLINE OF THE DEATH-RATE FROM EPIDEMICS

Perhaps the most striking example of the unexplained weakening of the death-rate at this time is provided by Hollingsworth's study of British ducal families. Their standard of nutrition could hardly have been less in the period 1680–1729 than between 1730 and 1779, and it is doubtful if industrial products such as cotton, iron, glass, pottery, and soap, which may have reduced the risks of growing sections of lower social orders could have affected their chances of life; nevertheless, the cohort of Hollingsworth's dukes who were born in the first period had an expectation of life of 34·7 for males and 33·7 for females. For those born in the second period, even though it includes the crisis years 1741–2, it was 45·8 and 48·2 respectively, that is, a rise of more than one-third (Glass and Eversley, p. 359). More surprisingly, the villages of Bedfordshire examined by Dr Tranter appear to have enjoyed a death-rate almost as favourable in the period 1730–79 (we have no information regarding the earlier period) as that of the English dukes and their offspring. The rates are given in Table 8 (Glass and Eversley, p. 362; Tranter, personal communication):

TABLE 8

Mortality of Infants and Young Persons, 1739–79

	percentage of deaths among recorded baptisms	
	under 5	under 21
British dukes (Hollingsworth)	20	27
Bedfordshire peasants (Tranter)	24	31

One other village, Fenny Compton, in Warwickshire, appears to have had an even more favourable survival rate. These rates are approximately comparable with similar rates for Northamptonshire county families obtained by Dr Razzell and are definitely better than those advanced by Mr Peller for the children of the European aristocracy. But the Bedfordshire villages must not be taken as typical; they must be regarded, probably, as exceptionally well favoured. At Wrangle in Lincolnshire, for instance, until the last decade of the century, 27 per cent of those baptized died before the age of 1 year; 39 per cent before the age of 5, and 60 per cent before the age of 21. Similar rates are found at Sleaford, and the infant death-rates at Clayworth in the seventeenth century were of the same order of magnitude (Tranter, 1966, pp. 189–202).

Discrepancies on this scale call for an explanation, and perhaps a clue can be found in the fact that both Wrangle and Sleaford were in the malaria zone of the English lowlands. Clayworth also was on the edge of the 'drowned lands' of north Nottinghamshire which formerly formed part of the submerged area of Hatfield Chase. The word malaria is unfamiliar to the student of English epidemiology; but if we call it by the homely name of ague, we shall have no difficulty in recognizing one of the killing diseases of pre-industrial England.

How far the ague can be identified with malaria, is, of course, a matter of dispute; but Creighton, in his *History of Epidemics* (ii. 300–3), shows that they have common characteristics, and one of particular interest in connection with the strange fall in the death-rate among the children of the dukes is that English ague, like Asiatic malaria, was susceptible to treatment by Peruvian bark or quinine. It was inefficiently administered until Dr Lind, in 1786, showed the importance of taking it in large doses; but Charles II had been sufficiently impressed by it to reward the famous quack, Robert Talbor, who administered it, with a knighthood, and sent him to his brother monarch, Louis XIV, where he acquired a fortune and a fabulous reputation (Creighton, ii. 319). When he died in 1682, he wrote his own epitaph in which he claimed to have saved the lives of many of the highest in the land, both in France and in England. Perhaps some of Hollingsworth's dukes' children and Razzell's gentry were among them.

In terms of numbers, the effects of this treatment would be marginal; at least until the 1780s, when the skill of Dr Lind brought it into general use for aguish complaints. A more important factor was probably drainage and enclosure of the many breeding grounds which was one of the consequences of the advancing frontier of improved agriculture in the seventeenth and eighteenth centuries. It is significant, in this connection, that the incidence of ague in Wrangle declined after enclosure and drainage in 1790 and that the author of the agricultural report for Derbyshire, in 1817, speaking of the enclosures which had contributed to the increase of numbers, also noted the disappearance of ague from the end of the century.

The use of Peruvian bark is perhaps the most important success to which the doctors can lay claim in the field of curative and preventive medicine; but in other fields, particularly in regard to the environmental factors affecting disease, they made important advances. We should not forget the enlightened treatment of the Quaker doctor, John Fothergill, during the epidemics of 1747–8, 1762, 1765, and 1782, involving an emphasis on fresh air, cleanliness, and a light diet. His rules for the clothing and feeding of infants represent a revolution in methods of child care among the well-to-do; and his recommendations for restful holidays at Matlock and Buxton for those suffering from consumption have a singularly modern sound. There were important publications in 1720, 1752, 1753, 1767, and 1785 which are said to represent collectively an immense advance in understanding the influence of environmental factors in infectious diseases. Whether these improved ideas were incorporated into medical practice on a sufficient scale to affect the death-rate is, however, open to doubt. In regard to hospital treatment, our two leading authorities, McKeown and Brown, are in no doubt at all. The chief indictment of hospital work, at this time, they say, 'is not that it did no good, but that it positively did harm' (Glass and Eversley, p. 291).

There were many local hospitals set up in the last quarter of the century, which were objects of pride to the founders and of comfort to the inhabitants; and to those of us who have made any study of the histories that they have usually left behind, these statements read very strangely. The Nottingham General Hospital, opened in 1782, claimed to have treated, by 1814, 10,913 in-patients and 28,954 out-patients, of whom a total of 27,300 were said to have been cured. Dr Chaloner has given a favourable account of the General Infirmary at Manchester where cod-liver oil was being administered to patients suffering from rickets in the 1780s (p. 55), while Professor Sigsworth goes further and attacks the whole structure of the McKeown and Brown thesis on the basis of the records of York County Hospital. There seems no doubt that in this matter they have overstated their case, and that far from being an ally of disease, the hospital system in the last quarter of the eighteenth century must be included among the factors that contributed to a decline of the death-rate. There is perhaps another department in which the achievements of the medical fraternity may have been underrated, that is, in respect of the practice of inoculation. We owe a renewed interest in this contentious subject to the researches of Dr Razzell, who, in a striking article in a recent number of the *Economic History Review*, reminds us that in the 1750s parish offices began to pay for inoculation as a cheaper alternative to looking after their infected poor. But it was not until the 1760s that the practice began to spread rapidly as a result of the cheap and comparatively safe methods evolved by apothecaries and local surgeons, under the lead of Robert Sutton, apothecary-surgeon of Framlington Earl (Norfolk), and his son Daniel Sutton. The essence of their success lay in attenuating the amount of the injection, so that the danger of infection with virulent smallpox was reduced to almost vanishing point. In the years 1760–8 they claimed to have inoculated 55,000 persons of whom only six had died. They set up partnerships with other surgeons and apothecaries and by 1776 the number of inoculations having been carried out was said to be upwards of 300,000. The practice spread more rapidly in rural areas than in towns and whole villages would submit to inoculation when outbreaks of smallpox threatened (pp. 317–18).

Is this the answer to our problem? Dr Razzell thinks that it is, and calculates that the number of lives saved by inoculation could account for the entire growth of population between 1750 and 1800 (pp. 328–9). Without going so far with Razzell we can say that inoculation must have contributed to the substantial fall of the death-rate of the village population at a time when prices were steadily rising, when the decay of domestic industry was thought to be a factor eroding the countryman's standard of living, and when the younger and more virile members of the rural population were being drawn off in increasing numbers to the towns. Some Nottinghamshire evidence is presented in Table 9:

TABLE 9

Nottinghamshire Death-rates in the Eighteenth Century

(i) *Village population* (Chambers, 1957, p. 55)

	Burials per thousand			
	1743	*1764*	*1801*	*1806*
Agricultural villages	27·5	26·0	18·1	17·5
Industrial villages	29·2	26·6	22·0	20·5

(ii) *Town of Nottingham* (Chambers, 1960, pp. 122–3)

Death-rates per thousand (burials × 1·10)

1740	1750	1760	1770	1780	1790	1795	1801
48·3	34·3	31·3	38·5	35·6	33·9	35·2	30·8

According to these figures—admittedly vulnerable but not inherently implausible—the death-rate in the agricultural villages fell by 33 per cent between 1743 and 1801, most of which occurred after 1764 when the death-rate still stood at 26·0. It is interesting to note that the death-rate of the industrial villages also stood at 26·6 in 1764, but by 1801 had fallen by somewhat less (17 per cent) to 22. In the town of Nottingham the death-rate in 1795 remained as high as 35·7 (higher by two points than in the first decade of the century); but by 1801 had fallen to 30·8, almost the whole of which can be accounted for by a fall of the child death-rate from 21·8 to 17·3 per thousand (Chambers, 1960, p. 122), and it was in 1800 that vaccination was introduced into the town of Nottingham. Briefly, it is possible that what vaccination did for Nottingham in 1800–1, inoculation had already done in the villages.

There are two problems arising out of this situation which I feel should not be overlooked. The first is the degree to which the decline in the impact of disease was due to the changing nature of the disease itself and to the part played by the factor of immunity, both on the part of those at risk and also on the part of the agents by which it was conveyed to its human victims. We have already noted that Hirst, in his book on the *Conquest of Plague*, attributed its disappearance not wholly to the victory of the brown rat over the black rat, important though that is, but also referred to the possibility of the development of rat immunity and the importance of a change in flea species.

The question that springs to mind at once is whether anything of the kind could have played a part in the declining virulence of other diseases in the eighteenth century. Two obvious fields for the operation of such a factor are in regard to smallpox and typhus. In the case of smallpox, it seems likely that natural immunity played an important part. On this subject Sir McFarlane Burnet has written an illuminating account (pp. 227–8). Smallpox, he says, reached epidemic proportions in 1628 and again in 1634, and while at this stage of its career it was relatively mild among children, and seldom fatal, it was especially dangerous to young adults. Its incidence increased until in London, in the eighteenth century, there was an average of 1,500 deaths a year. But by 1750, he thinks that practically every child born in London, or in the larger provincial towns, must have been exposed to the infection, which would surely tend to give immunity to those who survived early childhood. It then became almost entirely a disease of childhood where the level of immunity was at its lowest. Over 90 per cent of smallpox deaths in Manchester in 1769–74, Professor Burnet shows (p. 228), were of children aged under five. On the other hand, in a small Northamptonshire town in 1723–4 only 23 per cent were under five and a larger percentage over twenty. Hence, the greater incidence among adults and hence, it might be suggested, the greater prevalence in rural areas of inoculation noticed by Razzell compared with the practice in the great towns. With the spread of inoculation and then of vaccination immunity would be extended to the entire community. A student of epidemic history must, therefore, ask himself to what extent the decline of smallpox was a phenomenon of nature rather than the outcome of the ingenuity of man.

The second problem relates to the other scourge of the eighteenth century, typhus. Whether it was equal in importance to smallpox as a regulator of population growth need not detain us; but there seems no doubt that the very heavy death-roll in the 1680s and again in 1741–2 owed much to its ravages. It may have contributed to the visitation of 1728–9; it was more or less endemic throughout the eighteenth century, especially in crowded, insanitary areas, as is indicated by the names by which it was known—gaol fever, ship's fever, workhouse fever (Creighton, ii, ch. 1). It is rather remarkable that it was never known as factory fever, but there may be reasons for this as I shall show later. Typhus was also especially an urban disease associated with overcrowding, bad housing, and sanitation, and tended to become more frequent with the growth of urban congestion at the end of the century. Nevertheless, I think there is evidence that though the attacks may have been more numerous, their virulence tended to decline. In support of this, I would like to submit some inferential evidence drawn from the growth of town populations from their own natural increase. The records of four towns only are available—and these not in adequate detail—for this purpose. But if they may be taken as representative of the towns of England, it would seem that a demographic revolution was in progress even where the conditions of public health might lead one to expect it least. Towns had been proverbially the graveyard of successive generations of migrants, consumers of, rather than contributors to, the new growth that constantly flowed in from the surrounding country; but the experience of Nottingham, Exeter, Manchester, and London would suggest that from about 1750 this trend was checked and before the end of the century was put into reverse. The urban population, for the first time in its history, was on the point of recruiting itself by a normal annual increment from its own natural increase.

In Nottingham a favourable balance of baptism over burials began to emerge as a regular, though not uninterrupted, feature between 1750 and 1780, and after 1790 the gap widened to such effect that population grew almost as much by natural increase as by migration (Chambers, 1960, p. 122). In Exeter Pickard's evidence points to the 1750s as the beginning of an improvement in mortality (pp. 46–52), and although there were setbacks in the 1770s, as indeed there were everywhere, by the 1780s the margin of baptisms over burials was assured and permanent. In Manchester Chaloner tells us that there was a growing excess of births over deaths towards the end of the century, the average rising from 89 per year in 1765–7 to 370 in 1783–5 and to 674 in 1791 (p. 43). But the most spectacular change was to be found where it might be least expected, in London. Deane and Cole's statistics for the 'London area' (Middlesex, Kent, Surrey, Essex), show an excess of burials over baptisms of 568,000 for 1701–51 and 171,000 for 1751–81. These deficits gave way to positive natural increases of 81,000 for 1781–1801 and 525,000 for 1801–31 (p. 118). If attention is confined to Middlesex alone, the pace and timing of the improvement is qualified, but the general direction of the trend remains unmistakable. That county had deficits of 456,000, 177,000, and 18,000 for the first three periods mentioned, and the estimated natural increase for 1801–31 was 132,000 (p. 109). Yet in the midst of this obvious improvement, in the last decade of the century, prices were rising to famine heights.

Why did not disease strike with the same deadly effect as in the far less critical food crises of 1728–9 and 1740–1? There was, as might be expected, a visitation of typhus. Conditions were ideal—semi-starvation of townspeople, a six-week frost in 1796, overcrowding, and a total lack of sanitation. In Nottingham, a historian reported 'the gathered filth within doors is scattered daily in the dirty passages without . . . and many of these streets and lanes, if so they may be so-called, are without any sort of pavement, consequently without regulated water courses' (Chambers, 1960, p. 118). Under these conditions it is not surprising that in 1795 the death-rate rose to 35·2 per thousand, but in 1740, when the population of the town was only 11,000 compared to 28,000 in 1801 within the same area, it had risen to 48·3 per thousand (Chambers, 1960, p. 122). Why the relative mildness? Though immunity may not be ruled out it was far less efficacious in the case of typhus than in that of smallpox. We must therefore look to external factors to account for it: housing, drainage, domestic equipment, water supply, urban improvements, medical progress. But Nottingham was not in the van of progress in regard to any of these; in fact in regard to drainage and water supply it was probably getting worse owing to the crowded living conditions in the new courts and alleys and the increasing infection of the wells from which water was drawn. Only in one respect can Nottingham claim to have been leading the way: in the manufacture of cotton. Nottingham, of course, was a cotton town, the first in fact. Hargreaves and Arkwright had fled from Lancashire in 1768–9 and had initiated cotton-spinning by factory methods in Nottingham. Lancashire was second in the race, but quickly caught up. By the end of the century cotton hosiery, underwear, calicoes, bed-hangings, and sheets would be ousting those of wool; and cotton can be boiled, which is fatal for the typhus louse. The change to cotton would be especially beneficial to the poor of the large towns. Its significance for the populace of London has been described by Francis Place in unforgettable terms. Writing in 1829 of his memories of London over the previous sixty years he drew attention to two facts of special relevance in this assessment of typhus epidemics: first that fewer children had lice in their hair, and second that cotton garments and bed hangings, which were in wide use among the poor, were cheap and easily washed. He went on to say that he remembered the time when

the wives of journeymen, tradesmen and shopkeepers either wore leather stays, or what were called full-boned stays . . . These were never washed although worn day by day for years. The wives and grown daughters of tradesmen, and gentlemen even, wore petticoats of camblet, lined with dyed linen, stuffed with wool and horsehair and quilted, these were also worn until they were rotten.

A great change was produced by the manufacture of cotton goods.

These were found to be less expensive and as it was necessary to wash them, cleanliness followed almost as a matter of course . . . This very material change was not confined to the better sort of people as they were called . . . It descended, although rather slowly, to the very meanest of the people, all of whom as far as respects females, wear washing clothes . . . [the working classes are] more cleanly in their persons and their dwellings, than they were formerly, particularly the women, partly from the success of the cotton manufacture (George, pp. 71–2).

Drawing together this evidence, we have noted a remarkable improvement in the death-rate of the aristocracy and gentry and in that of London: a substantial fall of that of the agricultural and industrial villages, and a temporary fall in Nottingham in the 1750s and '60s, followed by a rise though not to the heights of the epidemic years of 1728–9, 1736, and 1741–2. Table 10 presents an estimate of the national trend:

TABLE 10

English Crude Rates, 1701–1830

(Deane and Cole, p. 127)

	1701–50	1751–80	1781–1800	1801–30
Death-rates	32·8	30·4	27·7	22·5
Birth-rates	33·8	37·2	37·5	36·9

If we are to accept the figures of Deane and Cole there was a national fall from 32·8 deaths per thousand population in 1701–1750 to 27·7 in the last twenty years of the eighteenth century. This was not evident in the north-west of England to any significant extent (28·0 per thousand to 27·0, according to the same authors), nor in the town of Nottingham; it may be that both areas reflected the results of a comparatively high birth-rate arising out of immigration, as well as overcrowding.

Table 10 also indicates that the chief fall appears to have occurred in the first three decades of the nineteenth century; but these figures have been severely challenged by Professor Krause on the grounds of the growing inadequacy of the parish registers. We shall have something more to say on this in the next chapter. In general, however, we can say, both in regard to the birth-rate as well as the death-rate, there was an inching forward in the sense of an improvement in both, leading to a change in the age structure illustrated by Figure 3. The fantastically jagged outline of the Lichfield chart for 1688 should be compared with the relatively symmetrically shaped national pyramid of 1791, showing the effects of the victory over epidemic disease which had worked such ravages on affected age groups in 1688. By 1791 there were not only more

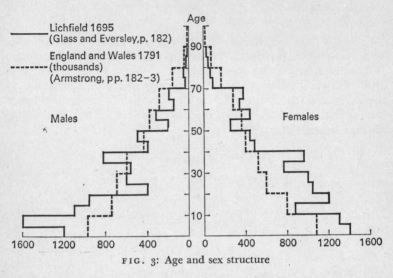

FIG. 3: Age and sex structure

births but also more survivals each year, with the result that each generation of those entering the marriage age was slightly larger than the last. The failure of disease to check this process of cumulative growth, as it obviously had done with savage effect in the past, is the most important single factor in the preparation for the demographic age which came to maturity in the nineteenth century and is still with us.

5

Bricks Without Straw : the Course of Population Change in the Eighteenth Century

In his examination of the various attempts made by students of eighteenth-century population change to interpret the very inadequate data at their disposal, Professor Glass refers to one of them as a skilful and ingenious attempt to make bricks without straw. This description would apply to all of them, and Glass has placed all subsequent students of the subject in his debt by the skill and ingenuity that he himself has brought to the elucidation of the methods that the pioneers of population study employed and the degree of credence that can be accorded to the results at which they arrived (Glass and Eversley, ch. 9). To attempt to retrace the path that Glass has blazed through this difficult statistical country would be an impertinence, especially as he himself promises a full-scale treatment of the problem of eighteenth-century population growth in a future publication of his own. Moreover, after pointing out the weaknesses in each of the estimates that he examines, he agrees that they are all of some value; and that 'if the object is to guess at the approximate size (within, say, a margin of 10–15 per cent) of the population of England and Wales at the beginning, middle and end of the eighteenth century, it may well be that they are all sufficiently near the truth to be accepted' (pp. 237–8).

The simplest, most familiar and, despite the criticisms that have been levelled against it, the most acceptable estimate is that of G. Talbot Griffith in his well-known book *Population Problems of the Age of Malthus* (p. 18). His figures are given in Table 11 overleaf:

TABLE 11

Population of England and Wales in millions

1700	*1710*	*1720*	*1730*	*1740*	*1750*
5·835	6·013	6·048	6·008	6·013	6·253

1760	*1770*	*1780*	*1790*	*1800*
6·665	7·124	7·581	8·216	9·168

The basis for this series is, of course, the inquiry undertaken by John Rickman in 1801 as a result of the controversy that was raging at the time, between the proponents of a rising and a falling population. It should be remembered that in 1783 the notable statistician Dr Price had estimated that the population of England had decreased by 1½ million since the revolution of 1688. He attributed this to the enclosures which had 'thrown down the cottages in the country with the result that the inhabitants fled to London and there were quickly corrupted by the vices and luxury of the capital so they soon perished'. This strange delusion, perpetuated by historians in regard to enclosures down to our own day, was so palpably in defiance of the observed facts that a stream of controversy was unloosed. Population study which had languished since the time of Gregory King suddenly took on a new lease of life, and information from a variety of sources, particularly the parish registers, began to be assembled which even now has not yet been properly assessed. The upshot of this new demographic interest consisted of two events of great and lasting importance to economic historians and demographers: the writing of the famous book by Thomas Malthus entitled *The Principle of Population as it affects the future of society* (1798) and the organization of the first census by John Rickman in 1801. The first of these is an example of what happens when learned fathers tend to pontificate on their pet subject in the hearing of their sons: the latter are either bored to death or stimulated to intellectual rebellion. The younger Malthus was stimulated to rebellion and woke up to find himself a famous man; and I think it is safe to say that he is as famous today as he was then. The work of John Rickman was a great deal less controversial but in some respects vastly more useful; and it is on his pioneer work of 1801 that much retrospective inquiry has been based.

This is not the place to refer at any length to the immense debt which students of population owe to the work of John Rickman. Almost single-handed he undertook the organization of the first census of the entire country, and in addition to this he initiated the study of eighteenth-century population by including in the schedule sent out to parish incumbents a question on the number of burials or baptisms in each parish for every tenth year between 1700 and 1780, and then for every year from 1781 to 1800. A return of marriages for every year since 1754 was also required (Flinn, p. 13). Needless to say the returns were by no means complete. There were wide gaps in the schedule owing to the haphazard way in which registers were kept and also owing probably to the carelessness with which the returns were in some cases compiled. Registers were known to get into private hands, their pages used for kettle-holders and wrapping paper, the entries themselves sometimes taken on scraps of paper and never entered into the registers at all. Rickman met these defects by substituting averages of preceding and succeeding years, but since the original returns appear to have been destroyed by an order of a departmental committee, it is no longer possible to go back to the original material and reconsider it.

Rickman himself used this material to make two estimates of population change in the eighteenth century, the first published in 1802 along with the census return of 1801, the second published after his death in the preface to the Enumeration Abstract of the 1841 census. Along with this was published another estimate by John Finlaison of the National Debt Office; a third was made by William Farr, of the General Registry Office and published in the 1861 census report. The dust was now allowed to settle both on the controversy and on the material on which it was based until 1913 when Professor Gonner published a pioneer study, followed in 1916 by Dr Brownlee's well-known article on 'The History of the Birth and Death Rates in England, taken as a whole from 1570 to the present time'. The Rickman figures were next used as a basis by G. T. Griffith in *Population Problems of the Age of Malthus,* first published in 1926. Griffith's book itself made history: it brought population study into the lecture rooms and transferred the central problems of eighteenth-century population from the pages of learned journals to the ordinary discourse of economic historians.

The problems raised by these various estimates are of two kinds,

one of method and one of interpretation. They centre on the difficulty of translating the entries of the registers into figures of births,
marriages, and deaths, and we will consider here only one of the
methods employed, namely that adopted by Griffith. First he found
a ratio that would raise the rates derived from the registers of
1825, 1830, and 1835 to those based on the registration of births
and deaths after the Registration Act of 1837. He found that by
raising burials by 10 per cent and baptisms by 15 per cent he could
bridge the gap between the figures of the old and the new system
of registration, and he then applied these ratios as constants for the
period from 1700 to 1840 (p. 16). The weaknesses of the system are
obvious; they are also common to a greater or lesser degree to all
competing estimates and are probably insurmountable, but they
give the best results at present available. There are two further
difficulties. First that up to 1780 the base figures are for decadal
years only and a line joining one decadal year to another cannot
have statistical value for anything that happened between them,
especially in view of the violent fluctuations of baptisms and burials
from year to year. A second difficulty is the increasing inadequacy
of the Anglican records in the eighteenth and early nineteenth centuries. So serious is this problem that one distinguished student of
the subject, Professor Krause, has mounted an attack upon the entire
structure of population study in the late eighteenth and early nineteenth centuries. He thinks that Anglican registration was adequate
until 1780, but after this it deteriorated markedly for the following
reasons: the imbalance between population density and the provision of churches, especially in the urban areas; the increase of plur-
alism and non-resident clergy with its problem of indifference to the
welfare of parishioners; the rapid spread of the revived dissenting
movements leading to hostility between Anglican and Dissenting
clergy, and above all the opening up of new nonconformist burial
grounds, which would mean, of course, that Anglican registers
would be deficient on burials. There was also the problem of
absentee Anglican parishioners during the period of the wars with
France, whose deaths would for the most part have appeared in
the church registers, and alongside this was the increased post-
ponement, and indeed neglect of, the practice of baptism, in the
towns. From 1820 the position, he thinks, improved, owing to the
revival of interest of Anglican clergy and the building of new
churches; but the shortfall of registration between 1800 and 1820

was, in Krause's view, on a sufficient scale to vitiate the entire structure of demographic generalization based upon the parish returns included in the official censuses of that period (Glass and Eversley, ch. 15). This is the explanation, he suggests, of the alleged fall of the death-rate of the early years of the nineteenth century and its reported rise after 1820; a statistical mirage which, he believes, has not only deluded subsequent students but deceived John Rickman himself. As a result of these objections Krause rejects the accepted trend of birth-rates and death-rates at the end of the century and substitutes his own, which he claims show not a fall of the death-rate but a rise of the birth-rate, as the most important factor in population growth during the period 1780–1820 (1958, pp. 69–70). The effect of Krause's criticism is not to provide straw for our brick-making, but to take away from us that which we have. However, since we are concerned only with the eighteenth century, and since Krause himself concedes that registration to 1780 was an acceptable reflection of births and deaths, we need not despair. Moreover, since in the villages the influences of the Church continued strong, and perhaps especially since Glass is willing to allow that the results derived from the registers may be regarded as within 10 or 15 per cent of the actual figures of population we can take heart and begin our attack upon the problem of interpreting the material we have.

First, let us consider the assumptions on which all these students of eighteenth-century population change have proceeded. They all appear, at least by implication, to regard the rate of growth of the first half of the century as representing the normal trend from medieval times and beyond: and assume a decisive break in the pattern *circa* 1750. Like Krause, they begin with 'the hypothesis that a demographic revolution occurred in West European contries roughly between 1750 and 1800' (1959, p. 164) The population explosion, in other words, is usually regarded as having made its appearance about 1750.

This hypothesis has recently been made the subject of an interesting study by Professor Tucker, which I will briefly summarize. In Figure 4, points D, E, and F represent Talbot Griffith's estimates of the population for 1700, 1750, and 1800, and by the simple device of extrapolating the 1700–50 rate of growth back to 1500, Tucker shows that we are brought to a figure of 4–5 millions in 1500 (A′). Most medievalists would agree that some 2.5–3.0 millions is a much more reasonable population figure for that early date (point A), and if they are right, it follows that the rate of growth of population for the whole or part of the period 1500–1700 must have been markedly higher than that estimated by Griffith for 1700–50—i.e. DE does not represent the pre-industrial growth rate but is in fact an aberration from it. Thus the year 1750 may be viewed not as a novel break with the past, but as marking a reversion to an earlier trend (pp. 210–11). Tucker goes on to suggest that the first thirty years of the second half of the century (1750–80) can be

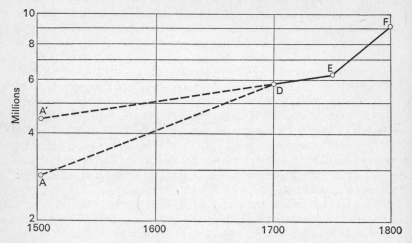

FIG. 4: Hypothetical population growth rates, 1500–1800 (After Tucker, p. 209)

thought of merely as a period of compensation for the abnormally low, even negative, growth rate implied for 1720–50 by Griffith's figures. He leaves us, therefore, with the implication that there is nothing unique about the upsurge of growth between 1750 and 1780; the character of abnormality was introduced only in the subsequent two decades when the compensatory movement (showing some signs of tapering off in the 1770s) was caught up by a new surge of population growth in the 1780s, marking the true break in the long-run trend (pp. 215–16).

This, however, is not quite the end of the implications to be drawn from Tucker's argument. He notes that Glass has tentatively reduced Gregory King's population figure of 5.5 million in 1695 to 5·2, and points out that this, taken in conjunction with Griffith's fall of population between 1720 and 1730 would imply that all the growth between 1700 and 1750 had taken place in the two sub-periods 1695–1720 and 1740–50, and that this would have required growth rates only fractionally lower than those for the period 1750–1780 (pp. 217–18). In other words, if we wish to find a parallel to the trend in the third quarter of the century we shall find it in that of the period 1690–1720, when population growth rates may have already been as high as during the first decades of the so-called 'vital revolution'.

I will now try to reveal the object of this somewhat tedious exercise. It is to relate these findings, based on the traditional materials—the strawless bricks about which Glass laments—to the results of the study of new materials derived from the parish registers. The first example is that provided by Professor Pentland's analysis of published parish-register material, which was referred to in Chapter 3. It will be remembered he found a high degree of consistency between the various series and a general long-term correspondence with the national series derived from Rickman. He then went on to look for differences over the short term and noted in particular that the parish series show a *greater* degree of fluctuation—a marked volatility—which is seen especially in the upward movement before 1720 and downward between 1720 and 1730, both of which have been indicated in the estimates based on Rickman. In terms of index numbers the discrepancy between the two series is shown in Table 12 (pp. 6–7):

TABLE 12

Comparison between Parish-Register Trends and Griffith's National Estimates

Natural increases (baptisms–burials), each based on indexes of 1740–1799 = 100

	Index for England and Wales (Griffith)	Index for 7 parish series
1700–9	34	84
1710–19	7	50
1720–9	−8	−26
1730–9	1	75
1740–9	46	28
(1740–99)	100	100

Briefly, Pentland's analysis highlights the substantial growth, in fact the demographic boom, occurring in the twenty or thirty years before 1720, as well as emphasizing the absolute check to population growth in 1720–9. Thereafter, his parish index suggests a buoyant recovery in the 1730s which is reflected in the national series only from the 1740s. Here it should be pointed out that Pentland's coverage is thin on urban communities—Leeds township is included, but not until 1735. Had he, for example, taken into account the decadal natural increases of Nottingham town (as distinct from the Nottinghamshire villages which are included), the effect would have been to have deepened the dip between 1720 and 1729 and somewhat delay the subsequent recovery, since it is known that Nottingham's rate of natural increase was also negative through the years 1725–44 (Chambers, 1960, p. 122). Here, at least, demographic recovery was not obvious until well after 1740, and perhaps one can think in terms of a twenty-year rather than a ten-year lag in growth after the upswing of the first two decades of the century.

May I now try to summarize the revision of the traditional pattern of eighteenth-century population growth for which this recent work on parish registers appears to call; briefly, it confirms a suspicion of Professor Glass about the base population figure of Gregory King and suggests that his reduction from 5.5 to 5.2 million or less in 1695 is in accordance with the facts; it shows that growth was taking place rapidly between 1690 and 1720—probably as rapidly as between 1750 and 1780. It tends to confirm Tucker's argument that 1750 was not so much a beginning of a new demographic age as a return to a previous trend and also that this new trend did not turn back on itself, but after a moment of hesitation in the late 1760s and again in the early 1780s went on to new heights. Perhaps this failure of the trend to turn back on itself in the 1760s and 1780s marks the decisive break between the new and the old demography.

We may now turn to another attempt to extract from the Rickman figures an intelligible pattern of what was happening behind the deceptive façade of the decadal totals. In their massive study, *British Economic Growth 1688–1950* (ch. 3), Deane and Cole rightly regard population growth as a vital ingredient in the process of industrialization, both in regard to labour supply and to market demand; they also quite properly realize that this can only be assessed realistically on a regional basis since the country was developing under regional stimuli which varied from place to place. They therefore take county totals of baptisms and burials as returned by Rickman; inflate them into births and deaths and group them by regions. These they present in the form of a series of regional rates of births and deaths and also of migration. Now let us admit that this is an impossible task with the material at their disposal, and they have been duly castigated for the many weaknesses with which their massive effort of statistical reconstruction is afflicted; but does anyone really regret that they made it? I believe, on the contrary, that so long as the figures are used to indicate broad trends and not to provide precise quantities they have performed a valuable service and have provided economic historians with a number of important tools with which to unlock some of the secrets of the period.

We may consider their findings from several angles: the contribution made by the urban recovery after the calamitous set-back of the period 1720–40; the continuous uninterrupted growth of the north and north-western counties before, as well as during the period of intense industrialization; the demographic upsurge in the agricultural counties in relation to the return of prosperity to agriculture after 1750; and the problem of the Poor Law.

In regard to the urban recovery, I have already drawn attention to the fact that as far as London and Nottingham are concerned the half-century mark represents something of a turning-point (see Chapter 4). Figure 5 gives the absolute natural increases for the two towns, London being crudely equated with Middlesex for this purpose. Now, if Nottingham is typical of provincial towns at the time, we can say that for them, the traditional picture challenged by Tucker still stands. The year 1750, or rather 1745, would remain the turning-point. For London, on the other hand, Deane and Cole's statistics suggest that inroads were made into the natural deficits after 1750, but that a positive balance, i.e. natural increases, was not achieved until after 1801. This agrees with the earlier findings of Dorothy George (p. 397), and we may conclude that in this respect the capital city (which contained nearly one-tenth of the entire population of England in 1801) lagged somewhat behind English provincial towns. In both, of course, the direction of the trend is unmistakable, and may be said to represent the dawning of a new urban demographic age.

E

(a)   London(=Middlesex)   (b)   Nottingham
      (Deane and Cole,p. 109)   (Chambers,1960,p.122)

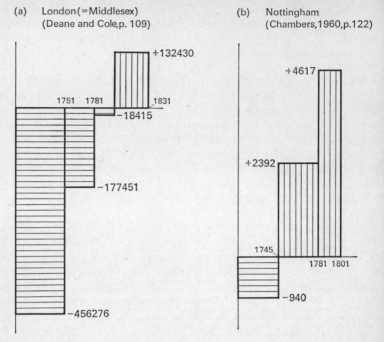

FIG. 5: Growth of population by natural increase in the eighteenth century

The precise timing and local variations of this pattern cry out for further research.

The next important conclusion to be derived from the Deane and Cole analysis of regional demography is the exceptional growth of the northern and north-western counties long before the conventional dates of the Industrial Revolution, which is sometimes thought to have brought these centres of population into being. On the contrary, the rate of growth was well above the national average for the first fifty years of the century and in fact, without its contribution to the national total, that period would have been not merely one of relative stagnation but of substantial net decline (see Table 13).

Among the interesting conclusions to be drawn from these figures is that the tradition that the industrial areas depended for their supply of labour upon the agricultural south and east

TABLE 13

Average Rates of Natural Increase and Migration,
1701–1830

(Deane and Cole, p. 127)

	Rates of natural increase per thousand				Rates of migration per thousand			
	1701–50	1751–80	1781–1800	1801–30	1701–50	1751–80	1781–1800	1801–30
north and north-west	4·8	10·6	11·3	15·1	−3·2	−2·0	−0·4	0·1
north-west	5·6	12·9	12·8	15·8	−3·4	−2·2	0·8	1·2
London area (4 counties)	−10·8	−4·8	2·7	8·2	11·4	11·4	9·6	7·4
south	2·2	7·6	11·2	16·5	−1·6	−2·8	−5·5	−3·3

is not merely untrue but the reverse of the truth. The reserve army of labour for the process of industrialization was provided not by the proletarianization of the peasantry and flight to the towns, but by the differential rate of growth of the industrial areas themselves, together with the adjacent agricultural districts. Indeed, it would appear that they were actually losing by migration until towards the end of the century.

Next we turn to the contribution made by the 'agricultural counties', defined by Deane and Cole as those where, in 1811, the majority of families drew their income from agriculture. (Eleven out of 16 of these are included among the southern counties in Table 13, and 11 out of the 18 southern counties are classed as agricultural.)

TABLE 14

Migration and Natural Increase of Agricultural Counties,
1701–1831

(absolute numbers)

(Deane and Cole, p. 108)

	1701–51	1751–81	1781–1801	1801–31
estimated natural increase	242,687	486,877	523,621	1,465,329
estimated loss by migration	−232,478	−113,826	−251,285	−379,044
estimated increase of population	10,209	373,051	272,336	1,086,285

Although the figures of Deane and Cole are only approximate, they suggest some interesting and important conclusions. Notice that in the first half of the century, the increase of population was only 10,209 whereas in the next thirty years population rose by over 370,000. This staggering difference calls for comment, however speculative, in relation to developments in economy and society at large.

A sharp set-back in population growth for the decade 1720–30 was followed by a period of low agricultural prices, which induced an agricultural depression, especially among the clay farmers of the Midlands. The fall in farmers' incomes would incline them to employ labourers who lived in, were usually unmarried, and who received their pay in the products of their own labour rather than cottage labourers who lived out and required a larger money wage for their subsistence. As Arthur Young said, when prices were low it paid farmers to employ men who lived in; when prices were high it was better that they should live out as cottage labourers, who paid for the provisions that they consumed. Also, by providing cheap grain for the distilling of gin, the agricultural depression exacerbated the demographic depression through the raising of the death-rate of London, and the greatest market of the country, serving one-tenth of the entire nation, was accordingly curtailed. As we see (Table 14), the agricultural counties were only able to absorb a mere 10,000 of their own natural increase in the first half-century, and nearly a quarter of a million found jobs elsewhere; no doubt many took the road to London and were numbered in the surplus of half a million deaths over births in that period. Eight agricultural counties are reported to have suffered an actual decline of population (Deane and Cole, p. 108). I would suggest in the light of this sequence of events that the demographic depression could be regarded as the largest single factor in the agricultural depression and must have had an adverse effect on the economy as a whole.

The acceleration in the growth of the agricultural population that followed, involving a doubling in the rate of natural increase and at the same time a halving of the number of emigrants, is a remarkable feature of the subsequent demographic situation which has not received the attention it deserves; and since, as we have shown already, there was a tendency for the agricultural death-rate to fall, one can see here the foundation of the rural demographic boom that was to follow. In the twenty years between 1780 and 1801 the total natural increase was over half a million, of which half found employment at home; and between 1801 and 1831 the tide of natural increase rose to nearly 1½ million, of which over 1 million stayed in their overcrowded villages (see Table 14).

May we not say that the demographic revolution was as much an agricultural and rural phenomenon as an industrial and urban one? Need we look further for the demographic crisis which so alarmed Malthus and his contemporaries? It had its roots in the rapid rural increase from 1750 onwards. The continued fall, especially after 1780, of the rural death-rate to which we have already referred provided a situation highly favourable for increased fertility as a result of fewer uncompleted marriages and a longer period of marital fertility. When to this is added the bonus effect of a relaxed Poor Law, we can see the dilemma in which a sensitive and humane observer like Malthus found himself; innate humanitarianism must be sacrificed to demographic necessity. The Poor Law must be cut back as the only alternative to demographic disaster.

How far was he right? That there was a rural demographic crisis is indisputable; the direct check of disease could no longer be counted on to effect a balance between supply and demand for labour; the direct checks of starvation, even Malthus conceded, could not be permitted; but to provide out of taxation forms of protection of infant life and incentives to procreate still further surplus lives, he devoutly believed, was a form of criminal folly both to the superfluous labourers themselves and ultimately to the nation as a whole. The mechanism by which the Poor Law might be expected to stimulate population operated through three agencies: direct support of wages under the Speenhamland system, allowances for large families, and subsidies for cottage rents. All these were classed as 'out-door relief' to the able-bodied; and it was these that Malthus proposed to abolish. It has, however, been recently argued that allowances had long been a feature of Poor Law administration in some areas in the first as well as the second half of the eighteenth century to relieve large families in distress, and when they were regularized by the Speenhamland system they were still so small as to provide no more than a basic subsistence. They would not, it was argued, provide in themselves an incentive for early marriage and larger families (Marshall, pp. 13–14, 42). On the other hand, the subsidizing of rents would no doubt promote cottage building in the open parishes; and the decline of living in, owing to the preference of farmers and their wives for cottage labour as the price of provisions rose, could hardly fail to promote earlier marriage. There was also, as we have shown already (Chapter 3), a substantial rise in illegitimacy for which lax Poor Law administration was held partly responsible. The only statistical evidence on this matter is that provided by Professor Krause in which he shows that the heavily pauperized counties—Bedfordshire, Buckinghamshire, Essex, Kent, Oxford, Suffolk, Sussex—had a census fertility ratio in 1821 of 643 children per thousand women between 15 to 49 against the average for England as a whole of 580. Sussex, the most heavily pauperized county, had a ratio of 721 (1958, p. 68). But we should also note that in the West Riding and other industrial areas the ratio stood at 677. Elsewhere, in the non-pauperized and non-industrialized counties the ratio must have been comparatively low. Moreover, the relatively high figure for the Speenhamland counties may well be due to the effect of Poor Law allowances in reducing infant mortality as a result of ante-natal and post-natal support for mother and child under the relief system, rather than in inducing conceptions before and after marriage: babies who would have died unrecorded without allowances survived as names in the baptism registers (Blaug, p. 174). Indeed, as Malthus freely admitted, the Poor Law was a double-edged agent; it acted as a deterrent as well as an encouragement to population through the system of closed parishes. Landlords could keep a rural paradise for themselves, uninfested by the offspring of their poorer neighbours, by refusing to build houses in their parishes and by drawing for their labour upon adjoining parishes. On balance, therefore, it seems safe to say that the effect of the Poor Law on population could only have been marginal. Malthus was not wrong, but in the demographic situation of the time, irrelevant, not to say socially mischievous in so far as his views moulded the worst features of the Poor Law Amendment Act of 1834. Even had the Poor Law done all that he attributed to it, it would still have caused only a mere eddy on the surface of the demographic tide. The essential feature in rural population growth was not the Poor Law; it was the changing age-structure consequent upon the fall in the death-rate and the demographic boom in the second half of the eighteenth century. Unfortunately, no analysis of the age-structure of the rural population has ever been carried out, as far as I know, but it has been shown by Dr Armstrong that

a significantly larger proportion of the population as a whole was in the 0–29 age-group in 1821 than in 1791 (64·7 per cent as against 56·7) ... both age distributions show a population which was predominantly composed of young people. In both cases every age group was substantially larger than the next older group. This was due not only to the effect of mortality in cutting down the generations as they passed through life, but also to the fact that the older groups were no doubt drawn from generations which had been at birth less numerous than the younger groups, i.e. to the fact that the total number of annual births was rising steadily. The predominance of the younger age groups in both 1791 and 1821 would necessarily keep the growth rate high in the following decades (pp. 139–41).

TABLE 15

Age Structure of the Population of England and Wales,
1791 and 1821
(per cent)

	1791	1821
0–9	23·8	27·5
10–19	18·5	20·8
20–9	14·4	16·4
30–59	38·4	32·4
70 and over	4·8	2·9
	99·9	100·0

And since the rural population to which this analysis of self-reinforcing growth especially applies still constituted until the last decade of the century 41 per cent of the entire labour force compared with 24 per cent in manufacturing industry, 11 per cent in trade and transport, 11 per cent in domestic and personal service, and 14 per cent in public, professional, and residual fields of employment (Armstrong, p. 150), we have some indication of the enormous part played by the fall in the rural death-rate in the second half of the eighteenth century.

I should now like to revert to Krause's dramatic rejection of the conventional rates of births and deaths. Did the national death-rate *remain*—as he argued—at a comparatively high level of 27 in 1811–20 instead of the 22 usually accepted, and did the national birth-rate stand at the very high level of 40 per thousand instead of the usual 34 (Krause, 1958, pp. 69–70: Griffith, pp. 28, 36), thus giving pre-eminence to the high birth-rate in the generation of population growth? As we have seen, in the case of the agricultural population the evidence is in favour of the traditional death-rate of 22 per thousand and an even lower birth-rate, in some parts, than the traditional estimate; while the high proportion of the agricultural population must give the influence of this sector a crucial weight in the balance of factors making for the final result. It is possible that Krause's rates are more appropriate for the *urban* population and to a lesser extent to the growing industrial districts of the Midlands and the north, where both birth-rates and death-rates were distinctly higher than in the rural areas. But all these trends had their roots in the upsurge commencing at the mid-century, which was essentially a phenomenon of the fall of the death-rate, temporary though this may have been in the case of some towns. Perhaps it is here that we must look, after all, for the turning-point in the demographic revolution: the years 1750–80 may have been, as Tucker argues, an example of compensatory upswing after a period of set-back: but the side-effects on the demographic and economic situation that followed were profound. On the demographic side it effected a change in the age structure of the population, which was carried on through successive generations: it became a younger population and therefore productive of higher fertility in the following years. The high birth-rates propounded by Krause were thus in all probability the reflection of a previous fall of the death-rate, and we need to recall the irrefutable logic of McKeown and Brown, that when birth- and death-rates are comparatively high, as they were at that time, 'it is very much easier to increase the population by reducing the death-rate than by increasing the birth-rate' (Glass and Eversley, p. 293).

Most important of all is the fact that these conditions, compensatory and therefore temporary as they may have been in origin, were not reversed in subsequent years, when critically high death-rates might have been expected to make a come-back as a result of a renewed epidemic cycle, or birth-rates might have been expected to show a decline as a result of imbalance between demographic and economic factors, for example, through slow erosion of employment opportunities as a result of increasing competition in the labour market. It is at this point that we re-enter the intricate and controversial area of the relation between the two processes of growth, the demographic and the economic. Are we to look to economic factors as the explanation of the break in the accustomed cycle of advance and retreat? Did the economy now take over and exercise a determining influence in the inauguration of a new demographic age? Or are we to regard the demographic cycle as an autonomous factor which changed its direction under influences that were non-economic in character and which itself played a decisive role in accelerating the upward trend to the climax that we call the Industrial Revoution, or the take-off into continuous growth?

I am not sure that these questions can be answered at present; but any attempt to do so would have to take into account the following considerations:

(1) The spontaneous and, as far as I know, unexplained growth of urban population by natural increase, as well as by migration. Nottingham grew by 40 per cent from natural increase in the second half of the century. London still required a flow of emigration to overtop the surplus of deaths, but natural increase was rapidly overhauling the deficit. Unfortunately, we do not know the proportion of growth by natural increase for other towns, but the over-all advance of the large industrial centres was on a very impresssive scale: Manchester rose from 9,000 to 102,000; Birmingham from 15,000 to 70,000; Glasgow increased by six or seven times in the course of this century. How much of this was dependent upon natural increase it is impossible to say. In so far as this growth reflected a regular surplus of births over deaths, we are witnessing a stimulus on the side of labour supply and market demand of an entirely new kind. We are unable to assess its dimension owing to the paucity of information on eighteenth-century urban growth: but we can be in no doubt that it played a significant role in triggering off the upsurge in the construction industries—housing, paving, bridge-building—with transferred effects to iron, coal, glass, paper, furnishing, domestic appliances, and the like, which is such a marked feature of these years. Of

London, Horace Walpole observed (Lewis, viii. 228): 'Rows of houses shoot out every way like a polypus; and so great is the rage of building everywhere, that if I stay [away] a fortnight . . . I look about to see if no new house is built since I went last'; whilst other contemporaries spoke of bricks being brought hot to the bricklayer, and of the growth of provincial cities such as Birmingham, Manchester, Hull or Liverpool, which 'would serve any King in Europe for a capital and would make the Emperor of Russia's mouth water'.

To this extent the fall in the death-rate had enabled the economy to gain another crucial rung in its upward climb to the take-off to sustained growth; and it acted as a catalyst in bringing about new combinations of existing factors of production.

(2) The quite remarkable surge of agricultural population to which I have drawn attention, and perhaps particularly the still more remarkable proportion that remained employed in agriculture, implies the existence of enhanced demand for the products of industry.

(3) The greatly increased consumption of food products, reflected in a rise of farmers' prosperity and a quite unprecedented spate of enclosures. Enclosure Bills totalled 25 in 1720–9, 39 in 1730–9, and 36 in 1740–9; in the four subsequent decades they attained 137, 283, 385, and 660 (Deane and Cole, p. 94). Enclosure by Act of Parliament often implied the partial rebuilding of villages; new farmhouses—many of them on a massive scale—labourers' cottages, roads, gates, fences, and so on. Visible evidence of rebuilding from 1750 can be seen on all sides in the brick and tile which is so characteristic of the Midlands. Most villages had their own brickyards but lime and coal had to be carted; and the rise in the number of Turnpike Acts from an annual average of eight in the first half of the century to about forty in 1750–70 (Deane, p. 71) is a measure of the pressure on coal supplies by market towns and villages now on the eve of the great Georgian rebuilding boom. The canals which had been talked about and were technically feasible in the seventeenth century now came into their own: two surveys were made for linking the Trent with the Mersey in the 1750s and then, in 1761, the breakthrough came where the pressure was beyond bearing: that is, to link the insatiable, demand for coal by the population of Manchester with the supplies from the Duke of Bridgewater's mines. The cycle in

agricultural and urban demographic growth had combined to effect the first phase in the revolution of transport.

(4) The industries that were given the fillip of new domestic demand by the spontaneous rise of population were the kind that invited capital investment, technological innovation, and entrepreneurial risk because they were price-elastic, being geared directly to the growing mass demand and susceptible to small changes of price. I am thinking, of course, of iron, glass, pottery, domestic utensils, but particularly of cotton. The local stockingers knew how to make cotton stockings on the stocking frame as early as 1730, but it was not until the 1750s that Nottingham began to catch the fever of cotton-spinning as the demographic recovery gathered strength. In 1758, Jedediah Strutt formed a partnership of small-scale hosiery manufacturers and launched the epoch-making Derby rib machine, which immediately stimulated a feverish experimental phase leading to the creation of machine-made lace, entirely a cotton product: and this demand for cotton was one of the factors attracting Arkwright and Hargreaves to Nottingham with results that are familiar to us all. All this could well have happened thirty years earlier, at the time of the abortive venture of Lewis Paul, but the expansive market of the 1760s was then lacking.

(5) The higher level of consumption which had been made possible by the fall of prices in the preceding period was not immediately eroded away by a swing in the reverse direction. The strength of the English agricultural industry was such that the new population could be fed mainly at the expense of exports, and the domestic price rose only slowly. Moreover, wages tended to rise rather than to fall because labour supply had not yet caught up with demand, and higher standards of consumption now spread among a generation of consumers which had been substantially reinforced by population growth. Perhaps there is something in the view that since the population was younger it was also more energetic and adventurous. I would certainly think that the atmosphere of buoyancy and high expectation to which entrepreneurs responded so readily would spread downwards to the lower orders; they had glimpses of a better world, and they left the local authorities in no uncertainty as to their displeasure by rioting when prices suddenly began to bite into their accustomed standards as a result of bad harvests in 1758–9 and 1765.

(6) The failure of high death-rates to return ensured that demographic pressure would be maintained. There were, of course, occasional grim reminders that the enemy of epidemic disease was still able to strike. Between 1765 and 1775 burials rose and in many villages overtopped baptisms. Marriages and births fell; and in 1782 there was an epidemic of influenza so severe that some local authorities took it as a return of the plague and issued handbills giving advice and warning to the people. Moreover, temporarily, most of the series of production showed a tendency to decline. Was there to be an anti-compensatory cycle that would check the rate of growth of population and thereby put a brake on economic expansion? As we know, the cyclical pattern did not in fact return, economic and demographic growth continued to oscillate around a rising trend, and the two variables were allowed to go forward in mutual stimulation in a fugue-like movement of reciprocal action and reaction into the nineteenth century. All these factors seem to me to stem directly from the spontaneous population growth having its roots in the recovery from the disastrous decade of 1720–30. On the other hand, we have to remember that population growth was a self-generating process, and that although the expansion of employment opportunities may sustain and stimulate an upturn that has already been initiated for non-economic reasons, as happened in the second half of the eighteenth century, the rate of growth may in some circumstances outstrip the need that called it into being by creating new generations of young parents more numerous than the last; and failing an extraneous factor such as the return to a high death-rate under the influence of epidemic disease, a crisis of relative over-population may result. The high death-rates did not, in the event, materialize and neither, in spite of Malthusian fears, did the crisis of over-population.

It is at this point, I think, we must admit that the economy was genuinely self-sustaining. The tide of population was on the flood but the economy was advancing still faster. For twenty years after about 1740 the rate of growth of total output rose, it has been estimated, at 1 per cent per annum, compared to 0·3 per cent in the previous period. It appears to have fallen back a little (to 0·7 per cent) subsequently, but in the last decades of the century, when population was forging ahead as never before, it was running at 1·8 per cent per annum (Deane and Cole, p. 80). There were still immense resources of land and capital available and the requisite technological skill and enterprise to develop them. There was therefore no danger that the impetuous flow of population would be brought up against a ceiling of stagnant output of food and shelter. At this point, we may say, the economy had become the senior partner in the combined process, a process which had now generated the necessary power to carry the nation over the divide that separated pre-industrial England from the modern world. How the combination came into being, how it operated in an essentially agrarian society, together with some indication of the rewards and penalties that its evolution involved, will be the subject of the concluding chapter.

6
Population and the economy in Pre-Industrial England: a summary view

WE have now surveyed the main outlines of the demographic pattern within which the economic forces of English society operated from the Middle Ages to the period of the Industrial Revolution. We have seen that the action between them was reciprocal: there was a pull of economic forces on population growth; but there was also a push of demographic forces on economic growth, and it is our task in this final chapter to consider the mechanism by which this reciprocal interaction was effected. Some of the attempts made to generalize this relationship have been probed in these pages, including the crude form of Malthusianism in which population is seen simply as a dependent variable reflecting food supply and employment opportunities, and the far more subtle and historically acceptable summary view in which the prudential check through fertility control by post-ponement of marriage is introduced. We have seen that some modern demographers go further and include also a degree of control within marriage through the spacing of births, either with a view to bringing back the population–resources equilibrium to a favourable balance, or perhaps, as Professors Thrupp and Chevalier suggest, reflecting a 'cultural' factor, an expression of rejection of life as it was lived in the terms of contemporary society. Dr Wrigley has assumed the former, although he suggests that it may have been instinctive, a form of automatic self-adjustment to external circumstances, derived from our animal ancestry which reduced fertility in such a way as to produce a point of balance between births and deaths some way short of the maximum possible. As a result the peasants of pre-industrial society effected their own salvation by 'homeostatic adjustment' of population numbers (1969, p. 140).

But population change was itself a profoundly important factor in economic change; neither was a mirror reflection of the other, and no easy formula employing the complete reciprocal relationship is possible. The demographic historian can, however, add something to the discussion of cause and effect by presenting examples from the past to probe the nature of the problem and to prepare for a more adequate formulation when demographic data allow. For one of the best documented examples we have to go outside the field of our present inquiry to the remarkable demographic experience of rural Pistoia, recently described so vividly by Professor Herlihy. The population (31,000 in 1244), had *already* begun to decline 'at least a century before the Black Death' to a level of 24,000; after this the fall was even more dramatic, to 9,000 in 1404, hardly more than a third of the 1244 level (p. 230). Accordingly, Herlihy finds substantial reasons for doubting whether the curve of population decline corresponds to a simple outline of a classical Malthusian crisis.

A precarious balance between population and resources . . . was a constant fact of Tuscan rural life as far back into the thirteenth century as our sources permit us to discern. The plagues and famines of the fourteenth century cannot therefore be considered Malthusian checks brought into play by and operating against a vigorously expanding population. These blows, for all their ferocity, only accelerated a movement of rural depopulation long in operation (p. 235).

Land hunger by a too numerous peasantry had led to exploitation by land owners, usury by capitalists, and heavy taxation by town authorities. The peasants, even before the Black Death, replied by refusing to marry, or if they married, to have children.

Daughters of the poorest families apparently had no hope of marriage. Those from a slightly more prosperous background had to await a turn in their father's fortunes, perhaps a good harvest, before their dowries could be paid and they could join their husbands . . . hard economic conditions seemed to have forced married couples to refrain from having children (p. 236).

The sequence of demographic boom and slump was reflected in the economy. Herlihy observes, quoting Professor Fiumi,

The stimulus which promoted the great medieval prosperity of the Tuscan towns was vigorous population growth in the countryside. By the middle and late thirteenth century, an exuberantly expanding population was forcing massive immigration into the cities and prompting entrepreneurship, experimentation and novel departure in all phases of urban life. As long as the challenge continued, the Tuscan cities remained large and strong and economically the wonders of Europe. After 1348, however, the demographic crash of the middle ages dissipated that challenge and decadence settled upon these once so thriving communities (p. 226).

The function of the Black Death was to accelerate a process that had already begun and to cut the golden cord that linked the splendour of the city with the squalor of the countryside. As numbers fell, high fixed rents gave place to flexible rents and share cropping. Landlords had to share the risks of enterprise; and while rents declined, outgoings in the form of agricultural investments by landlords increased and 'urban enterprise was starved of capital to help the countryside back to health'. A check was given to 'rent gouging' by landlords and exploitation by usurers, and Tuscany was given a stable basis at a subsistence level through share-cropping which has lasted virtually to the present day (pp. 243–4). In this case we may say that the worst that Malthus could imagine happened until the peasants took their own avoiding action by homeostatic adjustment at a lower level of population but a higher level of subsistence; yet the economy apparently was irretrievably damaged. The Pistoian episode cannot fail to prompt a number of questions in the historian's mind. At what point does a factor appear that provides for a reciprocal stimulation between town and country which could lead to mutual growth? Where and at what point does population growth result in a structure of demand that favours economic growth as a general principle of economic change? We know that the point was reached in England. Can the economic historian throw any light on how or when?

Something can be gained by comparing the experience of Pistoia with that of England before and after the Black Death. In demographic terms there is a striking resemblance: a phenomenal rise in population to the middle of the thirteenth century, and then a hiatus which eventually may well be shown to conceal a slowing down, though this is not yet fully established; then stagnation for a century followed by a recovery, not, however, on the basis of share-cropping but of yeoman farming within a tenurial system in which the landlord shared the risks with the tenant in such a way as to encourage the progressive exploitation of the soil to their mutual advantage. Far from urban capital being drained to nurse the countryside back to life, rural capital rose and flourished in equal and independent status alongside the growing urban centres. Landlords and yeomen expanded their activities together, and often at the expense of small farmers and labourers. There was a steady attrition of forest, moor, and fen, and by the end of the sixteenth century widespread experimentation in husbandry techniques. As Dr Jones has observed, 'that period looks to have been one in which inflationary profits were distributed from the labourer to the yeoman and to the landowner, to be spent on the "Great Rebuilding" of farms' (1967, p. 156). We should remember, too, that these innovating tendencies were operating within the specifically English context of freedom under the law, including freedom from arbitrary taxation. And when, in the seventeenth century, the landlords took upon themselves the burden of direct taxation in the form of the land-tax, the contrast with the continental system had gone full circle. Within this type of fiscal and agrarian structure, the growth of numbers implied the growth of potential consumers, and as a result of the agrarian improvements of the seventeenth and eighteenth centuries this potentiality was realized, with mass effective demand for the products of industry at last able to break through.

But this is only one side of the evolution that followed the crisis of the Black Death in England. There was also the industrial aspect, the features of which are less familiar and have indeed only recently been revealed on the demographic side. As in Pistoia, the thirteenth-century explosion of population was the essential condition for the expansion of the economy which blossomed in the high Middle Ages, making the thirteenth-century Renaissance such a paradox of glory resting on a foundation of popular misery. It provided rural entrepreneurs, i.e. manorial lords, with circulating capital in the form of human labour for expanded demesne farming, the production of surpluses for growing towns, and even for export. It also facilitated the mobilization of manorial and free labour for the immense building programme of monasteries, cathedrals, churches, and castles, which formed such a conspicuous feature of the history of this period. To what extent it would stimulate entrepreneurial activity in other spheres would depend on many considerations of which we know too little to generalize;

F

but it is a fact of some significance that the thirteenth-century 'Industrial Revolution' discovered some years ago by Professor Carus Wilson depended not only on water-power, but also upon the availability of labour on rural manors, where the fulling mills were set up. Professor Miller has recently gone somewhat further: after referring to the growth of exports of English cloth, especially Stamford's, in the twelfth century he writes (p. 68):

At the same time, growing population at home and the concentration of conspicuous wealth in the hands of great landowners and churchmen intensified demand for textiles of every quality. More people meant more customers for village weavers and town burellers; rich men at home and the export market offered opportunities for craftsmen, mainly settled in the great eastern towns, whose products compared favourably with those of any other part of Europe in the cloth market of Genoa.

When, however, the town industries began to feel the effects of competition as a result of 'the relatively mass-production methods of Flemish industry', and the advanced commercial techniques of the Flemish and Italian merchants (in the mid-thirteenth century), the incentive to exploit country cloth-making was given a keener edge. It was the cost differential of country industry in the over-populated villages rather than the introduction of the fulling mill that attracted industry to the countryside (pp. 76–7). Miller goes on to suggest that the recovery of the industry at the end of the century and in the early part of the fourteenth was due to the expansion of the cheaper lines of production developed on the basis of cheap village labour—'slump-products' he calls them—playing something of the same role in the fourteenth century as the new draperies played in the second half of the sixteenth.

Let us, however, consider the subsequent situation when the conditions were reversed and demographic collapse drastically altered the balance between labour and resources. Labour supply now became more crucial than ever; and it was during this period that the Tudor broadcloth manufacture assumed its traditional distribution. It has recently been shown that an important factor in this distribution was the existence of regional pockets of surplus labour arising from conditions of tenure or the availability of common land for settlement of migrant peasants. The details are given in the article by Dr Thirsk on 'Industries in the countryside' (Fisher, 1961), in which case after case is cited of textile industries establishing themselves in obedience to a pattern in which labour supply is the main determinant—more important than water supply or the availability of raw material or of markets. In some cases it was the existence of extensive commons or forest land that first invited settlement, and then attracted the commercial capitalists; in others—and indeed in most—it was the practice of equal partition of holdings which tended to proliferate communities of small farmers, among whom the link of kinship acted as a barrier to mobility and therefore contributed to their dependence upon subsidiary sources of income as their means of subsistence as holdings shrank through parcelization. Such centres as the Kentish Wealden forest villages, the Yorkshire Dales, the Westmorland Fells, are examples of the attraction of proliferating peasant communities made overpopulous by equal partition and therefore ripe for industrialization by the country capitalist; while on the other hand, Hertfordshire, a corn county of ancient settlement and with no room for new settlers, was found to be resistant to commercial penetration. The case of the broadcloth industry in Wealden Kent is especially interesting, both as to its rise and its fall. It was based, Dr Chalklin tells us, on a 'population denser than in most other parts of rural Kent, far larger than in fact the land could itself maintain'. The workers were farmers or labourers whose income from farming was too small to maintain them and their families; and its decline and disappearance in the eighteenth century seems to have been mainly due to the higher labour costs owing to the demand for labour of the London market, Kentish dockyards, and the fruit and hop gardens of central Kent (pp. 117, 122–3).

The differential advantage of labour supplies was crucial in the distribution of textile industries especially in the periods of general labour shortage. When labour was abundant the advantage was of course more widely diffused, so that old industries flourished and new ones took root. This is especially well seen in the second cycle of industrial and demographic growth to which Professor Nef once gave the name of the seventeenth-century Industrial Revolution. The upward movement of population probably began in the late fifteenth century. Rents and prices, in particular grain prices we are told (Phelps-Brown and Hopkins, 1957), ceased to fall from the third quarter of that century; and real wages began their long and relentless decline. It is pointed out that if real wages are expressed in terms of non-processed agricultural goods, there was a fall of no less than 60 per cent between 1510 and 1630; if expressed in processed agricultural goods the fall was less, perhaps 40–50 per cent. The difference was due to the fact that surplus population was seeking employment in industry, so keeping the labour element in costs down; and that owing to the relative inelasticity of agricultural production the increased demand from a rising population caused a disproportionate rise in the price of primary products and enabled farmers and landlords to enjoy highly favourable terms of trade with the towns. Professor Phelps-Brown and Miss Hopkins find that this situation was paralleled in France and other parts of Europe, and attribute it to an upward turn of population (pp. 290–1).

There were, of course, other contributory factors; war expenditure in the early 1540's and 1590's, dehoarding and the melting down of plate, and liberation of funds tied up in the decoration of churches and chantries, or paying for masses; but in a critical analysis on 'Profit Inflation and Industrial Growth', Professor Felix shows that the rise of prices was mainly concerned with agricultural products, while industrial prices rose comparatively little. He argues that this is consistent with the view that the lag of wages behind prices (which is alleged to have caused the profit inflation) relates rather to buoyancy in the labour market than to the intensity of the price rise (p. 462). However, he offers no empirical support for the supposition of population rise that his hypothesis requires.

Empirical support, in fact, is not lacking. Professor Hoskins's village of Wigston Magna, which had declined possibly by half between 1377 and 1450, was becoming 'populous and over-crowded' by the late sixteenth century. As Hoskins says, rather sadly, 'there were too many people in the place'. There were, in fact, about 80 families in the village in 1563, a rise of 30 per cent from the low point of 1450, and a return to the Domesday figure. Between 1563 and 1605 the number rose to 130 or 140 families, a rise of 60 per cent in forty years and nearly 100 per cent in a century (1957, pp. 59, 86, 171). He has cited evidence elsewhere (1953, pp. 55–7) of growth in other parts of England: in the Isle of Axholme, Plymouth, Bideford, Tiverton, and Birmingham, and attributes it rather strangely to improved housing and better food, though the proportion of the population who could have enjoyed these advantages must have been relatively small. Nor does he explain why these causes did not continue to operate with the same effect in the next century.

An examination of a number of parish registers appears to give a more precise chronology to this demographic boom. On the basis of current but unfinished work we have clear evidence of a large surplus of baptisms over burials in Bedfordshire villages from 1576. How far back the gap can be traced it is impossible to say as there are no registers available before that date, but that the surplus of baptisms over burials goes back some years would be suggested by the very strong upward trend of the former. As noted above, these were the years when Humphrey Gilbert said that England was pestered with people, when Hakluyt said that 'throughe oure longe peace and *seldome sickness* we are growen more populous than ever heretofore'; when London was said to have grown from 90,000 to 150,000 in forty years, and Lambarde could treat the growth of population as a matter of common knowledge.

It is clear, however, that the gap between baptisms and burials began to narrow in the last years of the sixteenth century, and by the third decade of the seventeenth century it virtually disappeared. The registers themselves are silent as to the cause, but it is well known that this was a period of plague and that smallpox also became widely dreaded. It had long been known by various names and in various forms, but it made its appearance in literature proper by being made the subject of a poem; a young man lamented the lost beauty of his lover as a result of an attack of smallpox, so the lover's loss is the historian's gain (Creighton, 1. 463). From now on the dread of this disease constantly recurs in domestic and literary records. There were other forms of fever too: in 1623 'a malignant spotted fever' began to take a heavy toll and the first week of September 1624 saw a total of 407 deaths in London, of which 250 were children; 'the mortality is spread far and near, and takes hold of whole households in many places' (i. 504–5). The dreaded scourge of plague, from which the country was never free, reached a new pitch of violence, and during the week ending 18 August 1625 the recorded deaths in London were 5,203, of which 4,463 were described as 'of plague'. The plague of 1625 was in fact 'a great national event although historians, as usual, do no more than notice it' (i. 509–11).

There were further mild outbreaks in 1630 and 1631; more severe and widespread occurrences in 1634–6 accompanied by fevers and smallpox; 1638 was a bad year for fevers and 1640–3 had 'exceptional mortalities, which plague alone can by no means account for'. Apparently the new affliction was typhus which was now in the early stages of its long and baleful career. Influenza was also at work, and referred to by contemporaries as 'the new disease'; no fewer than five epidemics were so called from 1643 to 1685 (i. 527–534.) The especially bad years were 1645–7, 1651, 1657–9, and 1661–5, not counting outbreaks of plague in 1645–7 and the Great Plague of 1665 (i. 555–77). Thereafter smallpox, typhus, and influenza took their toll with scarcely less effect until the last decade of the century when there is evidence that this scourge of disease was temporarily halted. In the early years of the century, writers had complained that the population was too large; but from the middle of the century the desirability of a larger population was voiced firmly and frequently, a change of attitude which can hardly be unconnected with the condition of public health under these repeated attacks of epidemic disease.

Once more the dip in the demographic curve put a scarcity value on labour, and where tenurial or inheritance customs provided a differential advantage in the search for lower labour costs, the putting-out capitalist was quick to take advantage of it. Dr Thirsk has pointed to the growth of the hand-knitting industry among the villages on the edge of Sherwood Forest and along the Nottinghamshire–Derbyshire border (p. 97), a movement which drew capital and entrepreneurial leadership not only from local towns but from London itself in the late seventeenth and early eighteenth centuries. The most significant of all these probings of commercial capital into the hinterland of the older settled areas was the penetration of Lancashire and the West Riding by the leaders of the cotton and worsted industries. The small family farms of Rossendale and other parts of Lancashire formed the root on which the local fustian industry was grafted; and as a result of differential labour costs the hard-thrusting petty clothiers of the West Riding were eventually able to triumph over the gentleman clothiers of East Anglia. Professor Stone (p. 32) has noted that there was a startling decline of immigrant apprentices into London from the north and west in the last quarter of the seventeenth century and wonders whether this could have been due to changing patterns of opportunity which kept them in their native counties.

This seems very probable in the light of the development of the textile industries there, but whatever the reasons, there is no doubt that these districts were on the move and that industry followed in the wake of demographic growth long before the conventional dates of the industrial revolution. The labour force for the industrialization of the north and west was self-generated; it primarily depended on its own fertility and on only short-distance migration (Deane and Cole, p. 117). That is not because the total amount of migration in the first half of the eighteenth century was small; on the contrary, it was relatively as large as in the second half, but it moved in the direction of London, not the industrial north. The industrial north had its own reservoirs to draw from, especially in the marginal areas of forest and upland such as Cumberland, Westmorland, Derbyshire, and the North and West Ridings where the natural increase rate in the first half of the eighteenth century was over 7 per thousand compared to a national rate of only 1·1. Professor Cairncross (p. 83) has said of the nineteenth-century mining communities, that they owed their growth not to immigration but to their own superior fertility, and the same is true of the northern and midland industrial areas long before. Certainly, the popular myth of a gadarene rush of uprooted peasants and domestic workers from the south to the north is not only untrue but unnecessary. The closely knit groups subsisting on minuscule holdings, or squatting on the margin of mountains and forest, responded to the opportunities which putting-out capitalists were anxious to provide and the results were mutually satisfactory.

One further comment on the alternating rhythm of expansion and contraction under the influence of population change may be made. It could be likened to a series of successive tidal movements, each reaching a higher flood level and then falling back, but to a level higher than it occupied before. Each upward and each downward movement left a characteristic deposit of entrepreneurial achievement: the upward movement of the thirteenth century left the experience of manorial high farming, urban industry, and ecclesiastical and royal buildings. The retreating tide threw up the yeoman farmers, a class of capitalist peasants, described by Professor Hoskins as 'men or families who could hang on in the face of adversity'; tougher peasants, like the Randulls who 'acquired the lands of their weaker fellows, the Swetings, and the Redleys', emerging as a peasant aristocracy, treading on the heels of the gentry (1957, pp. 141–2). It threw up also country capitalists who laid the foundations of the Tudor cloth industry; and the large-scale graziers who put farm to farm and village to village and turned large areas of deserted villages into sheep runs. Perhaps especially it raised *per capita* incomes so that an accumulation of spending power was able to provide an expanded market when the next upward movement of population gave the stimulus of cheap labour and growing demand to economic enterprise. The so-called industrial revolution of 1540–1640 thus derived some of its strength from the so-called Golden Age of the agricultural labourer that preceded it. The returning demographic tide of the late Tudor period was marked by a notable advance of metallurgical, glass, and coal production into which many aristocratic and squire-archical families plunged in haste, and not a few repented at leisure. Yet they helped to carry these industries to entirely new heights, and although they themselves often fell to ruin through their own fabulous over-spending on great houses and high living, they left behind permanent assets which could be developed by generations of smaller men—coal factors, iron masters, commercial middle-men—so to speak the yeoman class of industrial entrepreneurs—who had grown up under the shadow of the great Elizabethan leaders like the Talbots and the Willoughbys. The yeoman indus-trial leaders, such as the coal-owners Barber and Walker, and the Foleys in textiles, carried on with less panache but with greater tenacity and became the true fathers of the family firm of solid bourgeois tradition. But above all, the hard-fisted yeomanry of the fifteenth and sixteenth centuries turned into the innovating farmers and gentry of the seventeenth, who, alongside the aristocratic undertakers of the great drainage schemes and their co-adventurers, eventually brought into profitable use three-quarters of a million acres—half the modern area of the Fens—of land unsurpassed in productivity anywhere in these islands. By practising ley farming, the flooding of meadows and all the improvements described by Dr Kerridge, they accomplished the essential stages of an agricul-tural revolution which the eighteenth century had only to generalize as the practice of the entire country.

But there is another side of these conquests, borne forward on the tide of cheap labour. A price had to be paid, and it was paid by the wage-earning class, through their own power of self-recruited growth. It has been calculated that the rise of prices, occasioned mainly by population growth, reduced real wages by about 50 per cent in the course of the sixteenth century. The wage-earners, says Stone, were reduced to abject misery, which found intermittent relief in rioting and mob violence. He goes on:

excess supply of labour relative to demand not only increased unemployment, but forced down real wages to an alarming degree . . . the fall was undoubtedly of a magnitude for which there is no parallel in English history since the thirteenth century . . . [there was] a polarization of society into rich and poor: the upper classes became relatively more numerous and their real incomes rose; the poor also became more numerous and their real incomes fell (pp. 26–9, 49).

It should be remembered however, that this erosion of wages by rising prices was a slow process, taking place over a period of a century and a half; agricultural production was rising at the same time, and though women and children were said to be dying of lack of food in London streets, there is no evidence of the mass starvation, of hordes of people wandering from place to place in search of food and literally dying of hunger such as we read of on the continent of Europe, including France, and in Scotland. How far the advance of English farming was already widening the gap between the living standards in England and her continental neighbours cannot be measured, but other factors were making for the same end: the virtual absence of civil and foreign war on English soil; the astonishingly low level of taxation; the high degree of geographical and social mobility; the absence of tolls and regulations as barriers to exchange. As the sixteenth-century pamphleteer said, Englishmen had reason to count their blessings (see above, p. 56).

Yet infectious disease was no respecter of persons or of countries; and Englishmen seem to have been no more immune to it than their continental neighbours in spite of being better fed and better governed. Accordingly, while the boom in population continued until the end of the century and somewhat beyond, it was cut short in the end by the rough but effective surgery of epidemic disease. From 1625 or before nature again applied the brakes to demographic advance and they were not lifted until (I have suggested) the last decade of the century; or until 1750 if we are to follow the hypothesis of stagnation so sedulously promulgated by traditional authorities.

We might at this point pause to inquire what progress has been made in our search for the roots of the mass market from which the modern structure of industry springs. We can point to the proliferation of industrial villages, especially in periods of labour shortages, when local labour surpluses in remote villages provided a differential advantage over the towns in the distribution of domestic industry. We can point also to an agricultural community of solid yeomen farmers rising from a ruck of struggling subsistence peasants, and a substantial structure of landed gentry and urban commercial and professional classes, who, according to Stone, were almost on a level with the entire landed gentry in spending power. But the end of the search is by no means in sight, and we are fortunate in possessing a perceptive analysis which lays bare the nature of the obstacle that had still to be overcome. I am referring to the important article by Professor Coleman on 'Labour in the English Economy in the Seventeenth Century' in which he conducts a demographic analysis based on the data provided by Gregory King, of a society that had many of the potentialities of an advanced economy but was not destined to realize it for a century or more. He shows that the essential problem of this, in many ways, brilliant and successful society was the mass poverty on which it rested. On the basis of Hearth Tax data, King classed 23 per cent of the national population as 'labouring people and outservants' and another 24 per cent as 'cottagers and paupers', estimating that both groups had annual expenditures greater than their income. This means, in Coleman's view, that 'between a quarter and a half of the entire population were chronically below what contemporaries regarded as the official poverty line' (pp. 283–4). They were likely to remain so, for a number of reasons. First, owing to seasonal unemployment in agriculture and the dependence of other industries on wind and weather and commercial fluctuations, they were fully employed for less than half their time. They worked, it was suggested, about 150 days in the year; and with an expectation of life at birth of not more than 35 years, they had a short working life, burdened by the support of a high ratio of dependent children and to some small extent of old people incapable of work. There was therefore a constant pressure for higher wages; but paradoxically, owing to the absence of a conception of rising living standards through earning power alone, there was a marked preference for leisure over harder work for higher earnings. At the same time, both internal and external markets were expanding, and the competition of continental countries, especially in the textile industries, was growing rapidly (pp. 285–93). What was the answer? The modern prescription, Coleman says, would be a dose of fixed capital in the form of new and better machinery; but that was impossible because industrial technology was in certain essentials virtually stagnant. The only new inventions of note for more than a century had been the stocking frame, invented by William Lee the Calverton clergyman of Nottinghamshire, and the ribbon loom for making fancy woven products in the form of ribbons, in Lancashire; but though they were exceptions, and important exceptions, to the general rule of technological stagnation, they remained hand-machines dependent on the direct labour of operatives in their domestic workshops. The only way to increase production, therefore, was to increase the number of humanly operated machines within the traditional structure of industrial production. Circulating capital in the form of human labour remained by far the biggest factor of production. As Coleman says, 'qualitative improvement being virtually impossible, quantitative increase [of the existing means of production] had to suffice' (pp. 287–8). Hence the growing insistence upon the importance of a rise in population. Davenant, Childe, Petty, and Pollexfen all thought that large numbers with lower wages and lower prices was the answer.

It is my contention, as I have explained in an earlier chapter, that between 1690 and 1720 population in certain important areas of the country did, in fact, grow substantially. Professor Glass has suggested that the population in 1695 was 5·2 million, while the figure for 1720 is usually put at 6·047 million. That is to say, we must take account of up to 800,000 more mouths needing to be fed, bodies to be clothed and housed in 1720 than in 1690, and hands to turn the wheels of production to meet the needs of this expanding society. Such a rate of growth of population compares not unfavourably with that of 1750–80, the period, I have suggested, that provided the demographic and economic launching-pad, or spring-board, for the next, conclusive phase of sustained growth. Can we argue by analogy that the period of 1695–1720 was of the same character? In certain important respects it was: there was ample capital from the immense expansion of foreign trade or enterprise of all kinds; by the opening of the new century the capital and loan stock of the surviving companies totalled, it is calculated, over £10 million, double the figure for ten years before. A more significant measure of expansion was the doubling of the number of patents of invention in the last ten years of the century, i.e. 102 between 1690 and 1699 compared with 53 in the previous decade (Deane, p. 128); an advance which represents 'a surge of inventive talent' in Professor Wilson's expression (p. 371), and which was not destined to be repeated until after 1760. There was a boom in house-building and a great importation of timber which reached a high peak in 1709 in spite of the war; the construction of large buildings such as Blenheim Palace, several Oxford and Cambridge Colleges, a dock at Liverpool, and a Cloth Hall at Halifax, as well as many civic improvements such as paving, lighting of streets. In 1707 came the passing of the first Turnpike Act and a measure to regulate building in the metropolis, which perhaps suggests a brisk development in that industry, since the City Fathers were not often moved to corporate action on that level. The ending of the war in 1713 provided builders with additional labour supplies, and according to a contemporary, the number of new buildings in London was 'a full fifth of the whole in 1695'. There were further schemes for turnpiking, e.g. the Great North, the Holy Head, and other roads out of London; river improvements, enormously facilitated by the recent introduction of the pound lock; important developments in mining and a large expansion of the coal trade to London; and when the speculative wave receded it left behind something more solid than the worthless stock and irrecoverable debt that are usually associated with the collapse of the South Sea Bubble. There were also some very important technological windfalls left by the receding tide; the Darby iron-smelting process and the Newcomen atmospheric engine were the most outstanding in the field of metallurgy, but there were also important innovations in organization such as Ambrose Crowley's works at Newcastle, the remarkable silk mill at Derby, and an attempt to introduce large-scale workshop spinning and weaving at New Haddington in Scotland which at one time gave employment to 700 workers. There was a large expansion in coal consumption in industries other than building, such as brewing, glassmaking, soap and sugar, salt and alum. As a result of the development of the reverberatory furnace, the smelting of tin, lead, and copper, by means of coal, had become a practical proposition by the end of the seventeenth century, and the production of all these metals was rising; while if we are to find examples of expansion in the oldest industry of all, the textile industry, we must go to the ribbon looms of Lancashire where a tough and eager peasantry clutched at the opportunity to exploit the virtues of a machine on which a single workman could make 12 pieces of ribbon, 432 yards long, in two days. On the old narrow loom the same task would have required four men. Cockney weavers rioted against it and prevented its development in London, but Lancashire welcomed it; grouping workpeople in batches of half a dozen in a suitably sized workshop, under a substantial master-weaver, the leaders of the Lancashire cotton industry were already moving towards the form of a miniature factory system, though without power. A parallel development was the framework knitting industry, drawing commercial capital from London, which sought out the cheap labour of Nottingham and the villages on the verges of Sherwood Forest. We must not, of course, forget that the expansion of the period 1695–1720, like that between 1750 and 1780, presupposed a highly responsive agriculture which, in spite of frequent bad harvests and a rapidly rising population, was able to provide an export surplus of wheat, barley, and oats, even in the famine year of 1709–10. Indeed, it may be suggested that the parallel trend of high agricultural prices between 1708 and 1717, and the upward trend of all the statistical series of production between 1710 and 1720, was more than a coincidence. England was growing, and growing fast. In fact, Deane and Cole report that there are signs of movement of the economy at that time which contrast sharply with the stagnation of the second quarter of the century and they conclude: 'it is probable that most of the modest progress made in the first half of the eighteenth century took place in the first twenty to twenty-five years and that the movement was then checked for about twenty years' (p. 61). Average prices of cereals were also higher at the end of the seventeenth century and for the first two decades of the eighteenth, both absolutely and in relation to those of producer goods and consumer goods, than they were to be again for forty years; which suggests that economic expansion may have been helped by the prosperity of agriculture, all of which is consistent with the underlying assumption that I should wish to make of a rise in population.

How far is it possible to identify and explain the role of population change in this phase of economic advance? We have to consider first the fact that the stagnation, if not retreat, of population during the middle years of the seventeenth century coincided with a growth in aggregate production especially in agriculture and foreign trade. It should also be remembered that the demographic depression may have reflected not only the fortuitous action of disease but also the purposive action of family limitation: part of the 'homeostatic adjustment' spoken of by Dr Wrigley in defence of the standard of living. In either case, living standards would gain in view of the tendency of prices to fall. There would, we may presume, be a higher *per capita* income at the end than at the beginning of this period. Hence when population took its forward stride in the last decade of the seventeenth century it included a larger proportion of those with the means to satisfy their family demands at the higher level then ruling. This would represent an element of mass demand which would do something to neutralize the depressing effect of the resurgence of population which, judging by the outcry on the subject of poor relief, quickly manifested itself as a dead weight on the economy.

If Defoe is to be believed, the section that enjoyed a surplus would signify a great deal more than this. Of course, Defoe was nothing if not an enthusiast. He probably doubled the actual population of London in his description of that remarkable city; but even if we make appropriate allowance for pardonable exaggeration his estimate of mass demand is still large enough to warrant full citation. It is taken from the brilliant account given by Professor Landes who, after observing that the English labourer not only ate better but spent less of his income on food than his continental counterpart, and was reputed for wearing leather shoes when the Fleming or Frenchman wore clogs, quotes Defoe (1724) as follows (p. 281):

. . . for the rest, we see their Houses and Lodgings tolerably furnished, at least stuff'd well with useful and necessary household Goods: even those we call poor People, Journey-men, working and Pains-taking People do thus; they lye warm, live in Plenty, work hard, and [need] know no Want.

These are the People that carry off the Gross of your Consumption; 'tis for these your Markets are kept open late on *Saturday* nights; because they usually receive their Week's Wages late . . . in a Word, these are the Life of our whole Commerce, and all by their Multitude: Their Numbers are not Hundreds or Thousands, or Hundreds of Thousands, but Millions; 'tis by their Multitude, I say, that all the Wheels of Trade are set on Foot, the Manufacture and Produce of the Land and Sea, finished, cur'd, and fitted for the Markets Abroad; 'tis by the Largeness of their Gettings, that they are supported, and by the Largeness of their Number the whole Country is supported; by their Wages they are able to live plentifully, and it is by their expensive, generous, free way of living, that the Home Consumption is rais'd to such a Bulk, as well of our own, as of foreign Production . . .

Is it possible that under certain hypothetical conditions a massive dose of fixed capital, as suggested by Coleman, could have enlarged the element of mass demand and absorbed the remaining unassimiliated surplus of unemployed and unemployable of which he speaks? Only the emergence of a leading sector, such as a revolutionized cotton manufacture, could have answered the question. Ambrose Crowley's iron works at Newcastle and the silk mill at Derby pointed the way, but the economic base of each was too narrow, and the cotton industry, which was predestined to play the part, had scarcely yet achieved a life of its own. In any case, the question was not put. Nature intervened and cut off a large section of the home market by the last of her periodical prunings; and London compounded with Nature by indulging in the gin orgy.

I have already suggested that the check to population that was given by these agencies had a role to play. It improved the condition of the diminished labour force and may well have induced in it a rudimentary conception of a rising standard of life. This may not have been difficult, for as Landes points out, English society was an open, not a rigid, society and one of the complaints against the poor was that they dressed to be indistinguishable from their betters (p. 283). Professor John has suggested that the expectations of most classes had increased since the Restoration (1961, p. 190), and it is reasonable to suppose that another 'golden age of the labourer' from 1720 to 1750 would bring even the poorest to raise their sights.

Alongside the various signs of demographic retreat, it is not difficult to find evidence that the rate of economic growth also began to recede. Building in London almost came to an end by 1730; the oft-mooted project for another bridge across the Thames faltered and petered out. Turnpiking almost stopped, and enclosures by act slowed down to a trickle; the output of industrial goods seems to have become virtually stationary; the export trade revived, but there was no corresponding increase in the total of industrial output, and in some sections, notably mining and metal industries, the supply of goods on the home market seems to have dropped sharply. Thomas Lombe's silk mill at Derby, which is said to have cost £30,000 in 1717, was sold for a mere £3,800 in 1731; and stocking frames that had come pouring into Nottingham from London in the first quarter of the century were found to be redundant, a drag on the market, and some were broken up for scrap. What was the limiting factor in this process of expansion? It was not the absence of technological innovation. Darby's smelting of iron by coke was available but not widely used; Kay's flying shuttle, of 1730, was not brought into general use for another thirty years. The application of the stocking frame in the manufacture of cotton hose, in the same year, made virtually no impact until the '50's; while the remarkable technological breakthrough by Lewis Paul in the power-spinning of cotton failed, largely it would seem, through undisciplined workmen taking advantage of the shortness of labour. 'Not half my people came to work today', he said in 1742 'and I have no fascination in the prospect I have to put myself in the power of such people' (Ashton, p. 211), whilst according to a contemporary account the factory at Northampton had five frames set up but barely hands enough to keep four at work. The water wheel was capable of making 15 revolutions a minute but the workers generally flooded it bringing the rate down to 6 or 8 revolutions. As a result of the failure of Lewis Paul's enterprise the hand-spinning of cotton was given a further thirty-year lease of life; but it is a fact worth noting that when Hargreaves and Arkwright came to Nottingham in 1767–8 they are not reported to have complained either as to quantity or quality of labour, nor labour of them. Arkwright was an astute manager of labour, organizing works outings and the like; and when his factory was burned down in 1771, the workpeople are said to have stood round in dumb misery, which may have represented something more than sorrow at losing their jobs. By this time, of course, the upward thrust of population after 1750 had introduced an element of competition, and new products such as cotton stockings (originally introduced in 1730) and machine-made lace evoked an atmosphere of emulation and induced a fever of inventive ingenuity among the manufacturing artisans; and had put an end to twenty or thirty years of frustrated innovation in textiles.

With respect to the iron industry, its relatively slow progress may be due in some measure to technological shortcomings; but it has been noted that iron exports were disproportionately high at a time when 'nearly all the production indicators record a period of comparative stagnation ... It seems probable that almost the whole of the increase of output of wrought iron was sent abroad during this period' (Deane and Cole, p. 58). The stagnation of printed textiles to which the same authors also call attention (p. 54) can hardly be attributed to any other cause than the inelastic home demand reflecting the check to population growth; and its striking revival from the 1750s can plausibly be associated with the removal of this brake upon production as a result of the upturn of the demographic trend. In the case of agriculture, depression fell upon the clay farmers and surplus grain was syphoned off into exports or absorbed by the gin industry in London; and their troubles were exacerbated by competition with the light-soil farmers of Norfolk and elsewhere who reacted to the challenge of low prices by increased production with the aid of advanced techniques; but in so far as low prices had a depressing effect on investment in the clay areas, the consumption of industrial goods was curtailed.

These remarks should not be taken to imply that this was a period of general industrial depression; for the working population in town and country—especially cottage labourers—were enjoying a halcyon period, which was enough to prevent that. But the tempo of expansion seems undeniably to have somewhat fallen compared to the 1690–1720 period. Farmers may have exercised a restraint on it by employing labourers living in, rather than the more expensive (and prolific) cottage labourers; and there is evidence that some agricultural counties actually declined in population between 1700 and 1750 (Deane and Cole, p. 103). Moreover, Malthus maintained that the stagnation of population reflected the postponement of marriage by labourers anxious to maintain their unaccustomed high standards; but more credible explanations are not far to seek.

The upward turn of prices from about 1750, reflecting the flood of population that had been gathering since the high birth-rates of the '30s and temporarily checked by the typhus epidemic of 1740–1, brought new prosperity to farmers and landlords and stimulated a wave of investment in enclosures, new buildings, and transport improvements, contributing thereby to the astonishing expansion of the third quarter of the eighteenth century. It was in the character of the English economy at this time that industry, agriculture, and the flow of investment could respond to such a stimulus. Population change was working in double harness with agricultural innovation; a head of power was generated that, aided by a concurrent boom in the European and American trading areas, took the economy over the hump to the great turbulent stage of sustained growth. All forms of enterprise, including the heavy growth industries, were stirred to new life, and the failure of the threatened return of the epidemic cycle in the 1770s to materialize marks the climactic point in the power of the alliance of demographic and economic forces to effect a fundamental change. The fortuitous element in population growth—epidemic disease—could no longer intervene by visitations involving overwhelming mortality which checked demand, reduced the labour force, and enhanced the preference for leisure on the part of the survivors. As the population rose, the great reservoir of internal demand rose with it. When Arthur Young made his national income calculation in 1770 he produced a figure that implied a doubling of average real income since 1688; and 'there is not much doubt', say Deane and Cole, 'that the widespread improvements and innovations in agriculture, transport and industry helped to maintain if not to increase real incomes per head in the last quarter of the century' (p. 97).

In no part of the country was the transition so radical and so sustained as in the north-western counties. For reasons that are far from clear, they appear to have escaped the demographic setback of the second quarter of the century and enjoyed the singular good fortune of rising money wages as well as rising population and falling prices. Here indeed is an example to support Professor John's statement: 'Perhaps the unique importance of the years 1680–1750 lies in the emergence, for the first time, of a situation in which the terms of trade between manufactures and primary products turned in favour of the former for reasons other than a fall in population. Until then, the major variable had been the size of population' (1961, p. 187). But it is my contention that elsewhere population remained the major variable until the second half of the century; then, the advance of industry, agriculture, and transport acquired such momentum that the advance of population could be absorbed and made to provide a stimulus of increased production and increased consumption. In the case of the north-western counties this had apparently been true from the beginning of the eighteenth century and probably before. A comfortable surplus by natural increase had kept them well ahead of the rest of the nation, and it can hardly be doubted that the long period of expanding numbers along with rising real and money wages and low prices inaugurated the beginning of a new age for the labour-ing poor as well as for the entrepreneurial middle classes of Lancashire, Cheshire, the West Midlands, and the West Riding. Here was the forcing ground of the Industrial Revolution, to be joined from the 1740s by the East Midlands and from the 1770s by South Wales, and there is some evidence that the labouring poor began to regard themselves—and to be regarded by others—as an integral and indispensable part of the economic process. They had experienced a substantial improvement in the standard of living and they organized themselves through their eighteenth-century combinations of workmen to maintain it. They were activated by the push of competition in the expanding labour market and also by the pull of increased supplies of articles of mass consumption—pots, pans, clothes, especially cotton clothes, houses. There was both a need and a desire to increase production; and Adam Smith observed that the problem among piece-workers was not that they were idle but that they were liable to do themselves an injury through overworking for higher pay. One aspect of the Industrial Revolution that is often overlooked is that the labour force was not only very much larger but that it was worked very much harder. Increased output was not due entirely to new technology but increasing effort by those working in the traditional industries played its part. There is even a report that farm workers of East Anglia trotted back to the harvest field with their wagons, a comment that, to anyone familiar with the ways of horse-drawn farm wagons, is difficult to believe; but the fact that it was made is not without significance.

Difficult as it is to determine the gains and losses in terms of economic and social well-being, there is no doubt that this rise in numbers did not prove, as Malthus feared it might, to be a barrier to further economic advance; and while large groups like the agricultural labourers and skilled domestic workers may have lost previous qualitative advantages in their traditional way of life, there was a large and increasing proportion who found opportunities to improve their lot and were becoming integrated into the developing industrial society. The nascent working-class movement, though it focuses attention on the evils that it encountered and tried to remedy, is itself a sign of changing times in that it was considering taking steps to become a recognized part of the political nation. By the turn of the century, the growing self-respect and self-confidence of some sections of the London working men was a subject of comment. A foreign visitor, writing of London in 1810–11, said: 'There is an ambition in parents to give a better education to their children than they have received themselves . . . and such is the proper sense every individual entertains of his rank as a man that there is not one so low as to suffer the treatment he would have borne in former times' (George, p. 308). The abject poverty of the lowest substratum of the London population, which had been a feature of London life hitherto, was also being slowly worn away: in 1825, Place wrote:

There is not now one beggar where there were ten or even twice ten. We are no longer tormented by regular vagabonds who make themselves loathesome objects in the streets. Those who were not old enough . . . to have noticed the beggars in the streets, can scarcely believe it possible that they should have existed in such large numbers, and can form no conception whatever of the horribly disgusting state in which they were (George, p. 212).

The vicious circle of self-perpetuating poverty was at last on the point of being broken: the process was not completed in the eighteenth century and it may be that the danger of a relapse was not finally surmounted until railways and steam-shipping had drawn the heavy industries and engineering to full stature and had opened up new markets of illimitable potential throughout the world. But if danger there was, it arose, it seems to me, not from a relapse into over-population and Malthusian miseries, such as were afflicting Ireland and the Celtic fringe, but rather from the opposite; from a sudden return to pre-industrial death-rates which would have decimated the labour force and brought the economic advance to a stop, as a result of the curtailment of labour supply and domestic demand. Perhaps we should not leave this subject without paying a final tribute to the permissive role of the micro-biological world. The plague had ceased, we are told, because from

1728 the brown rat had chased out the black rat from the habita-
tions of men in Western Europe, and the free-roaming flea that
had afflicted mankind with plague bacillus was exchanged for a
nest-loving flea which apparently disliked the flavour of human
blood. If this is true, it is perhaps the most gigantic example of
good luck in the recorded history of mankind: the dietetic pecu-
liarities of the free-ranging flea, apparently enabled the Industrial
Revolution to proceed on its way.

We have noted that a rather less improbable explanation has
been advanced by the author of *The Conquest of Plague*; but in
either case, the fate of industrial society was deeply involved in
a fortuitous decision of nature, since there was nothing in the
armoury of Victorian Science to prevent the *materies morbi* of
plague from performing the same prodigies of destruction with
which it had assailed the peasants of the fourteenth century if it
had been in the right biological posture to do so. As M. Henry has
said, 'we still do not know whether this reduction in disasters [in
the eighteenth century] was produced by man, the result for
instance of economic progress, or whether it was just a piece of
good luck, the continuation of which was made possible by the
undeniable progress of a later period' (Glass and Eversley, p. 448).
Coming from a scholar of M. Henry's stature, this is a statement
on which economic historians should ponder before they can claim
to have found the roots of the Industrial Revolution.

Bibliography

THE primary object of this bibliography is to list the sources and authorities referred to in the text. All references to studies published in D. V. Glass and D. E. C. Eversley, *Population in history* (1965), are given individual entries here and, where appropriate, the original place of publication is indicated. In the text, references are given to the Glass and Eversley pagination, except in the case of Professor Chambers's own studies of the demography of the Vale of Trent (1957) and Nottingham town (1960).

It will also serve as a further reading list, and to enhance its usefulness in this respect, a number of publications not specifically referred to by Professor Chambers have been added. One of these is E. A. Wrigley, ed., *An introduction to English historical demography* (1966), and it should be noted that all references to Wrigley (1966) in the main body of the text refer to this author's article, 'Family limitation in pre-industrial England', published in the same year.

W. A. A.

ARMSTRONG, W. A., (1965) 'La Population de l'Angleterre et du Pays de Galles 1789–1815', *Annales de démographie historique*, 2 (Paris).

ASHTON, T. S., (1955) *An Economic history of England: the eighteenth century* (Methuen, London).

BEAN, J. M. W., (1963) 'Plague, population and economic decline in the later Middle Ages', *Economic History Review*, 2nd ser., 15.

BENNET, H. S., (1965) *Life on the English manor: a study of peasant conditions 1150–1400* (C.U.P.).

BLACKER, J. G. C., (1957) 'Social ambitions of the bourgeoisie in eighteenth-century France, and their relation to family limitation', *Population Studies*, 11.

BLAUG, M., (1963) 'The myth of the Old Poor Law and the making of the New', *Journal of Economic History*, 24.

BLUNDELL, M., (1952) *Blundell's diary and letter book, 1702–28* (University Press, Liverpool).

BRENNER, Y. S., (1969) *A short history of economic progress* (Cass, London).

BROWNLEE, J., (1916) 'The history of the birth- and death-rates in England and Wales, taken as a whole from 1570 to the present time', *Public Health*, 29 (Cambridge).

BUER, M. C., (1926) *Health, wealth and population in the early days of the industrial revolution* (Routledge, London).

BURNET, F. MACFARLANE, (1962) *Natural history of infectious disease* (C.U.P.).

CAIRNCROSS, A. K., (1953) *Home and foreign investment, 1870–1913* (C.U.P.).

CARUS-WILSON, E., (1941) 'An industrial revolution in the thirteenth century', *Economic History Review*, 1st ser., 11.

CHALKLIN, C. W., (1965) *Seventeenth century Kent: a social and economic history* (Longmans, London).

CHALONER, W. H., (1959) 'Manchester in the latter half of the eighteenth century', *Bulletin of the John Rylands Library*, 42 (Manchester)

CHAMBERS, J. D., (1957) *The Vale of Trent, 1670–1800: a regional study of economic change.* Supplement 3 to *Economic History Review*; or, short abstract in Glass and Eversley, q.v.

——, (1960) 'Population change in a provincial town: Nottingham 1700–1800', in L. S. Pressnell, ed., *Studies in the Industrial Revolution* (Athlone, London): or, short abstract in Glass and Eversley, q.v.

CHEVALIER, L., (1965) 'Towards a history of population' in Glass and Eversley, q. v.: or, *Population* (Paris, 1946).

CLAY, C., (1968) 'Marriage, inheritance and the rise of large estates in England, 1660–1815', *Economic History Review*, 2nd ser., 21.

COLEMAN, D. C., (1958) 'Labour in the English economy of the seventeenth century', *Economic History Review*, 2nd ser., 8.

CORNWALL, J., (1970) 'English population in the early sixteenth century', *Economic History Review*, 2nd ser., 23.

COULTON, G. C., (1925) *The medieval village* (C.U.P.).

COX, J. C., (1910) *The parish registers of England* (Methuen, London).

CREIGHTON, C., (1965) *A history of epidemics in Britain* (2 vols), 2nd edn (Cass, London).

DAEDALUS, (1968) *Historical population studies* (volume 97, spring number) (Cambridge, Mass.).

DEANE, P., (1965) *The first industrial revolution* (C.U.P.).

DEANE, P., and COLE, W. A., (1962) *British economic growth 1688–1959* (C.U.P.).

DRAKE, M., (1962) 'An elementary exercise in parish register demography', *Economic History Review*, 2nd ser., 14.

EKWALL, E., (1956) *Studies on the population of medieval London* (Almquist and Wicksell, Stockholm).

EVERITT, A., (1967) 'The marketing of agricultural produce', in THIRSK, J., (1967), q.v.

EVERSLEY, D. E. C., (1965) 'A survey of population in an area of Worcestershire from 1660 to 1850 on the basis of parish registers' in Glass and Eversley, q.v.; or *Population Studies*, 10, 1957.

——, (1965) 'Population, economy and society', in Glass and Eversley, q.v.

——, (1967) 'The home market and economic growth in England, 1750–80', in Jones and Mingay, q.v.

FELIX, D., (1956) 'Profit inflation and industrial growth', *Quarterly Journal of Economics*, 70.

FISHER, F. J., (1957) 'The dark age of English economic history', *Economica*, New ser., 24.

——, (1961) *Essays in the economic and social history of Tudor and Stuart England* (C.U.P.).

——, (1965) 'Influenza and inflation in Tudor England', *Economic History Review*, 2nd ser., 18.

FLINN, M. W., (1966) *The origins of the Indusrial Revolution* (Longmans, London).

——, (1970) *British population growth, 1700–1850* (Macmillan, London).

GEORGE, M. D., (1965) *London life in the eighteenth century*, 2nd edn (Penguin, Harmondsworth).

GLASS, D. V., ed. (1953) *Introduction to Malthus* (Watts, London).

——, (1965) 'Population and population movements in England and Wales, 1700–1850', in Glass and Eversley, q.v.

——, (1965) 'Two papers on Gregory King', in Glass and Eversley, q.v.: or *Population Studies*, 2 (1950) and *Eugenics Review* (1946).

GLASS, D. V., and EVERSLEY, D. E. C., eds (1965) *Population in History* (Arnold, London).

GONNER, E. C. K., (1913) 'The population of England in the eighteenth century', *Journal of the Royal Statistical Society*, 76.

GOUBERT, P., (1952) 'En Beauvais: problèmes démographiques de XVIIᵉ siècle', *Annales: économies, sociétés, civilizations*, 7 (Paris).

——, (1956) 'The French peasantry of the seventeenth century: a regional example', *Past and Present*, 10.

——, (1968) 'Legitimate fecundity and infant mortality in France during the eighteenth century: a comparison', *Daedalus*, 97, q.v.

GREENWOOD, M., (1935) *Epidemics and crowd diseases* (Williams and Norgate, London).

GRIFFITH, G. T., (1967) *Population problems of the age of Malthus*, 2nd edn (Cass, London).

HABAKKUK, H. J., (1950) 'Marriage settlements in the eighteenth century', *Transactions of the Royal Historical Society*, 4th ser., 32.

——, (1958) 'Population growth and economic development', in *Lectures on Economic development*, Istanbul University.

——, (1963) 'Population problems and European economic development in the late eighteenth and early nineteenth centuries', *American Economic Review*, 53, Papers and Proceedings.

——, (1965) 'The economic history of modern Britain', in Glass and Eversley, q.v.; or, *Journal of Economic History*, 18 (1958).

——, (1965) 'English population in the eighteenth century', in Glass and Eversley, q.v.; or *Economic History Review*, 2nd ser., 6 (1953).

HAIR, P. E. H., (1966) 'Bridal pregnancy in rural England in earlier centuries', *Population Studies*, 20.

HAJNAL, J., (1965) 'European marriage patterns in perspective', in Glass and Eversley, q.v.

HALLAM, H. E., (1958) 'Some thirteenth century censuses', *Economic History Review*, 2nd ser., 10.

HARE, R., (1967) *An outline of bacteriology and immunity*, 3rd edn (Longmans, London).

HARTWELL, R. M., (1967) *The causes of the Industrial Revolution* (Methuen, London).

HECKSHER, E. F., (1954) *An Economic History of Sweden* (Harvard U.P., Cambridge, Mass.).

HELLEINER, K. F., (1965) 'The vital revolution reconsidered', in Glass and Eversley, q.v.; or, *Canadian Journal of Economics and Political Science*, 23 (1957).

HENRY, L., (1965) 'The population of France in the eighteenth century', in Glass and Eversley, q.v.

HERLIHY, D., (1965) 'Population, plague and social change in rural Pistoia, 1201–1430', *Economic History Review*, 2nd ser., 18.

HIRST, L. F., (1953) *The conquest of plague* (Clarendon Press, Oxford).

HOLLINGSWORTH, T. H., (1964) 'The demography of the British peerage', *Population Studies*, 18 (Supplement)

——, (1965) 'A demographic study of British ducal families', in Glass and Eversley, q.v.; or *Population Studies*, 11 (1957).

——, (1969) *Historical demography* (Hodder and Stoughton, London).

HOMANS, G. C., (1942) *English villagers of the thirteenth century* (Harvard U.P., Cambridge, Mass.).

HOPKINS, M. K., (1965) 'The age of Roman girls at marriage', *Population Studies*, 18.

HOSELITZ, B. F., (1957) 'Population pressure, industrialization and social mobility', *Population Studies*, 11.

HOSKINS, W. G., (1953) 'The rebuilding of rural England, 1570–1640', *Past and Present*, 4.

——, (1964) 'Epidemics in English history', *The Listener*, 31 Dec.

——, (1968) 'Harvest fluctuations and English economic history, 1620–1759', *Agricultural History Review*, 16.

HUZEL, J., (1969) 'Malthus, the Poor Law, and population in early nineteenth century England', *Economic History Review*, 2nd ser., 22.

JOHN, A. H., (1961) 'Aspects of English economic growth in the first half of the eighteenth century', *Economica*, new ser., 28.

——, (1967) 'Agricultural productivity and economic growth in England, 1700–1760—postscript', in Jones (1967), q.v.

JONES, E. L., ed., (1967) *Agriculture and economic growth in England, 1650–1815* (Methuen, London).

JONES, E. L., and MINGAY, G. E., eds (1967) *Land, labour and population in the Industrial Revolution: essays presented to J. D. Chambers* (Arnold, London).

JUTIKKALA, E., and KAUPPINEN, M., (1971) 'The structure of mortality during catastrophic years in a pre-industrial society', *Population Studies*, 25.

KERRIDGE, E., (1967) *The Agricultural Revolution* (Allen and Unwin, London).

KRAUSE, J. T., (1958) 'Changes in English fertility and mortality, 1781–1850', *Economic History Review*, 2nd ser., 11.

——, (1959) 'Some implications of recent work in historical demography', *Comparative Studies in Society and History*, 1.

——, (1965) 'The changing adequacy of English registration, 1690–1837', in Glass and Eversley, q.v.

——, (1967) 'Some aspects of population change, 1690–1790', in Jones and Mingay, q.v.

LANDES, D. S., (1965) 'Technological change and industrial development in Western Europe, 1750–1914', in H. J. Habakkuk and M. M. Postan, eds, *Cambridge Economic History of Europe, VI, The Industrial Revolutions and after* (C.U.P.).

LASLETT, P., (1965) *The world we have lost* (Methuen, London).

——, (1969) 'Size and structure of the household in England over three centuries', *Population Studies*, 23.

LASLETT, P., and HARRISON, J., (1963) 'Clayworth and Cogenhoe' in H. E. Bell and R. L. Ollard, eds, *Historical Essays, 1600–1750* (Black, London).

LEWIS, W. S., (1937) *Horace Walpole's correspondence*, 34 vols, ongoing (O.U.P.).

LORIMER, F., (1954) *Culture and human fertility: a study of the relation of cultural conditions to human fertility in non-industrial and transitional societies* (Unesco, Paris).

LOSCHKY, D. J., and KRIER, D. F., (1969) 'Income and family size in three eighteenth century Lancashire parishes: a reconstitution study', *Journal of Economic History*, 29.

MARSHALL, J. D., (1968) *The Old Poor Law, 1795–1834* (Macmillan, London).

MCKEOWN, T., and BROWN, R. G., (1965), 'Medical evidence related to English population changes in the eighteenth century', in Glass and Eversley, q.v.; or *Population Studies*, 9 (1955).

MILLER, E., (1965) 'The fortunes of the English textile industry in the thirteenth century', *Economic History Review*, 2nd ser., 18.

NEF, J. U., (1934) 'The progress of technology, and the growth of large-scale industry in Great Britain, 1540–1640', *Economic History Review*, 1st ser., 5.

PENTLAND, H. C., (1965) 'Population and labour supply: England in the eighteenth century', unpublished paper: Third International Conference of Economic History, Munich.

PEYTON, S. A., (1915) 'The village population in the Tudor Lay Subsidy Rolls', *English Historical Review*, 30.

PHELPS-BROWN, E. H., and HOPKINS, S. V., (1957) 'Wage-rates and prices: evidence for population pressure in the sixteenth century', *Economica*, new ser., 24.

PICKARD, R., (1947) *Population and epidemics of Exeter in pre-census times* (Townsend, Exeter).

POLLARD, S. and CROSSLEY, D. W., (1968) *The wealth of Britain* (Batsford, London).

POSTAN, M. M., and TITOW, J., 'Heriots and prices on Winchester manors', *Economic History Review*, 2nd Ser., 11.

POUND, J. F., (1962) 'An Elizabethan census of the poor', *University of Birmingham Historical Journal*, 8.

RAFTIS, J. A., (1964) *Tenure and mobility: studies in the social history of the medieval English village* (Pontifical Institute of Medieval Studies, Toronto).

RAZZELL, P., (1965) 'Population change in eighteenth-century England: a reappraisal', *Economic History Review*, 2nd ser., 18.

——, (1967) 'Population growth and economic change in eighteenth and early nineteenth-century England and Ireland', in Jones and Mingay, q.v.

ROSTOW, W. W., ed. (1963) *The economics of take-off into sustained growth* (Macmillan, London).

RUSSELL, J. C., (1948) *British medieval population* (University of New Mexico Press, Albuquerque).

SALTMARSH, J., (1941) 'Plague and economic decline in England in the later Middle Ages', *Cambridge Historical Journal*, 7.

SHREWSBURY, J. F. D., (1970) *A history of bubonic plague in the British Isles* (C.U.P.).

SIGSWORTH, E. M., (1966) 'A provincial hospital in the eighteenth and early nineteenth centuries', *The College of General Practitioners' Yorkshire Faculty Journal*, June.

SKIPP, V. H. T., (1963) *Discovering Bickenhill* (Department of Extra-Mural Studies, University of Birmingham).

SMITH, K., (1951) *The Malthusian controversy* (Routledge and Kegan Paul, London).

SOGNER, S., (1963) 'Aspects of the demographic situation in seventeen parishes in Shropshire, 1711–60', *Population Studies*, 17.

STONE, L., (1966) 'Social mobility in England, 1500–1700', *Past and Present*, 33.

THIRSK, J., (1961) 'Industries in the countryside', in Fisher (1961), q.v.

——, ed., (1967) *The Agrarian history of England and Wales, IV, 1500–1640* (C.U.P.).

THRUPP, S., (1965) 'The problem of replacement-rates in the medieval English population', *Economic History Review*, 2nd ser., 18.

TRANTER, N. L., (1966) 'Demographic change in Bedfordshire 1670–1800'. Unpublished Ph.D. thesis, University of Nottingham.

——, (1967) 'Population and social structure in a Bedfordshire parish: the Cardington list of inhabitants, 1782', *Population Studies*, 21.

TUCKER, G. S. L., (1963) 'English pre-industrial population trends', *Economic History Review*, 2nd ser., 16.

ULE, G. U., (1925) 'The growth of population and the factors which control it', *Journal of the Royal Statistical Society*, 88.

UTTERSTROM, G., (1965) 'Two essays on population in eighteenth century Scandinavia', in Glass and Eversley, q.v.

VAN BATH, B. H. S., (1963) *The agrarian history of Western Europe, A.D. 500–1850* (Arnold, London).

VINCENT, P. E., (1947) 'French demography in the eighteenth century', *Population Studies*, 1.

WATT, I., (1957) *The rise of the novel* (Chatto and Windus, London).

WATTS, D. G., (1967) 'A model for the early fourteenth century', *Economic History Review*, 2nd ser., 20.

WESTERMARCK, E., (1901) *History of human marriage*, 3rd edn (Macmillan, London).

WILLIAMS, O., (1911) *Life and letters of John Rickman* (Constable, London).

WILSON, C., (1965) *England's apprenticeship, 1603–1763* (Longmans, London).

WRIGLEY, E. A., (1966) 'Family limitation in pre-industrial England',
Economic History Review, 2nd ser., 19.
——, ed., (1966) *An introduction to English historical demography*
(Weidenfeld and Nicolson, London).
——, (1969) *Population and history* (Weidenfeld and Nicolson, London).
YOUNG, A., (1788) *A tour in Ireland*, 2 vols (Whitestone, Dublin).
ZIEGLER, P., (1969) *The Black Death* (Collins, London).

Index